PRAY FIRST

SIMPLE STEPS FOR TALKING (AND LISTENING) TO GOD

FOR YOUNG READERS

CHRIS HODGES
ILLUSTRATED BY GERALDINE SY

Tommy NELSON®

An Imprint of Thomas Nelson
thomasnelson.com

Pray First for Young Readers

Copyright © 2025 by Chris Hodges

Tommy Nelson, PO Box 141000, Nashville, TN 37214

All rights reserved. No portion of this book may be reproduced, stored in a retrieval system, or transmitted in any form or by any means—electronic, mechanical, photocopy, recording, scanning, or other—except for brief quotations in critical reviews or articles, without the prior written permission of the publisher.

Published in Nashville, Tennessee, by Tommy Nelson. Tommy Nelson is an imprint of Thomas Nelson. Thomas Nelson is a registered trademark of HarperCollins Christian Publishing, Inc.

Published in association with Yates & Yates, www.yates2.com. The Writer is represented by Cyle Young of C.Y.L.E. (Cyle Young Literary Elite, LLC), a literary agency.

Tommy Nelson titles may be purchased in bulk for educational, business, fundraising, or sales promotional use. For information, please email SpecialMarkets@ThomasNelson.com.

Unless otherwise noted, Scripture quotations are taken from the International Children's Bible®. Copyright © 1986, 1988, 1999 by Thomas Nelson. Used by permission. All rights reserved.

Scripture quotations marked MSG are taken from The Message. Copyright © 1993, 2002, 2018 by Eugene H. Peterson. Used by permission of NavPress. All rights reserved. Represented by Tyndale House Publishers, Inc.

Scripture quotations marked NIV are taken from the Holy Bible, New International Version®, NIV®. Copyright © 1973, 1978, 1984, 2011 by Biblica, Inc.® Used by permission of Zondervan. All rights reserved worldwide. www.zondervan.com. The "NIV" and "New International Version" are trademarks registered in the United States Patent and Trademark Office by Biblica, Inc.®

Scripture quotations marked NKJV are taken from the New King James Version®. Copyright © 1982 by Thomas Nelson. Used by permission. All rights reserved.

Scripture quotations marked NLT are taken from the Holy Bible, New Living Translation. Copyright © 1996, 2004, 2015 by Tyndale House Foundation. Used by permission of Tyndale House Publishers, Carol Stream, Illinois 60188. All rights reserved.

ISBN 978-1-4002-5350-0 (audiobook)
ISBN 978-1-4002-5348-7 (eBook)
ISBN 978-1-4002-5347-0 (TP)

Library of Congress Cataloging-in-Publication Data

Names: Hodges, Chris (Pastor), author. | Sy, Geraldine, illustrator.
Title: Pray first for young readers : simple steps for talking (and listening) to God / Chris Hodges ; illustrated by Geraldine Sy.
Description: Nashville, TN : Tommy Nelson, [2025] | Includes bibliographical references. | Audience: Ages 8-12 | Summary: "This fun guidebook on prayer will have children and tweens turning to God before going to anyone or anything else! In Pray First for Young Readers, bestselling author and pastor Chris Hodges shows that praying is simple yet powerful when you know God as your Friend, Father, and Savior"-- Provided by publisher.
Identifiers: LCCN 2025003518 (print) | LCCN 2025003519 (ebook) | ISBN 9781400253470 (paperback) | ISBN 9781400253487 (epub)
Subjects: LCSH: Prayer--Christianity--Juvenile literature. | Prayers--Juvenile literature.
Classification: LCC BV212 .H634 2025 (print) | LCC BV212 (ebook) | DDC 248.3/2--dc23/eng/20250219
LC record available at https://lccn.loc.gov/2025003518
LC ebook record available at https://lccn.loc.gov/2025003519

Printed in the United States of America

25 26 27 28 29 LBC 5 4 3 2 1

Mfr: PC/LSC / Crawfordsville, IN / June 2025 / PO #12285290

This book is dedicated to my grandchildren: Jackson, Andy, Rhett, Ryser, Ethan, Caleb, Charlotte, Carolina, Rowan, and Jane.

May this book inspire you to seek the beauty of prayer and to walk closely with God each day.

With all of my heart,
Papa

CONTENTS

PART 1. WHAT IS PRAYER? — 1

Chapter 1. Why Pray? — 3
Chapter 2. Where and When to Pray — 13
Chapter 3. What to Pray — 23
Chapter 4. The How of Prayer — 33
Chapter 5. The Who of Prayer — 45

PART 2. PRAYERS TO HELP YOU PRAY — 58

Chapter 6. The Prayer of Jesus — 61
Chapter 7. The Prayer of Moses — 73
Chapter 8. The Prayer of Jabez — 85
Chapter 9. The Prayer of the Sheep — 95
Chapter 10. The Prayers for the Lost — 107
Chapter 11. The Prayers for Battle — 117
Chapter 12. The Prayer for You — 127

PART 3. PRAYER + FASTING = SUPERCHARGED PRAYERS — 136

Chapter 13. Fasting? What's That?..139

Chapter 14. What Are FAQs About Fasting?...149

Chapter 15. How Did People in the Bible Fast?....................................159

Chapter 16. 21 Days of Prayer and Fasting..169

Chapter 17. Do You Have Your Shield?..189

ACKNOWLEDGMENTS — 195

NOTES — 197

PART 1

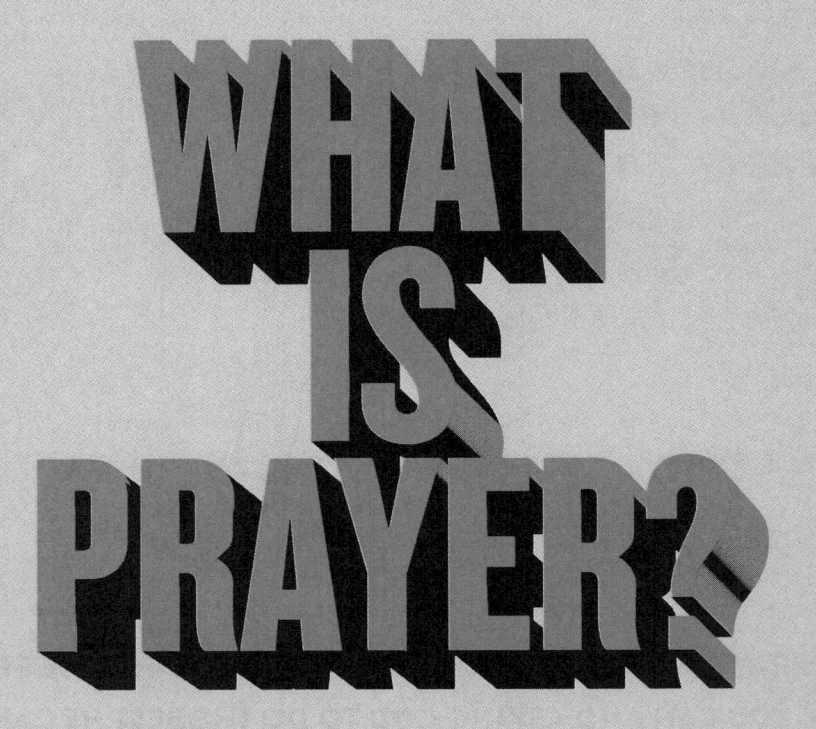

WHAT IS PRAYER?

LET'S TALK ABOUT PRAYER

Chances are, you've heard the word *prayer* before. Maybe from your family or friends. Maybe from church. But maybe you aren't sure exactly what it means or how to do it. (It's okay. Plenty of grown-ups are confused about it too.)

Prayer is a big deal. So big that this entire book is about it. But what exactly is prayer?

PRAYER IS THE DIFFERENCE BETWEEN DOING THE BEST *YOU* CAN AND ASKING GOD TO DO THE BEST *HE* CAN.

Here's a definition: Prayer is simply talking to and listening to God.

The definition is simple, but it reveals a truth so amazing that it's almost unbelievable. *Almost.*

Want to know what it is? Turn the page and find out!

CHAPTER 1
WHY PRAY?

PRAYER IS EASIER THAN YOU THINK.

WHAT IS THE AMAZING TRUTH ABOUT PRAYER?

God wants to talk to you.

Yes, *that* God!

The same One who made mountains and meerkats, oceans and avocados, and endless snowflakes and unending galaxies. He wants to have a conversation *with you*. And those conversations have the power to change your life.

It's a fact: Writing something down helps you remember it. So write the words *God wants to talk to me!* all around the edges of this page. How many times can you squeeze them in? Bonus points if it's more than ten!

PRAYER: talking to and listening to God

BUT I'M NOT A GROWN-UP—CAN I STILL PRAY?

The answer to that question is yes! Double yes!! Triple yes!!!

It doesn't matter how old you are. God wants to hear from *you*. He is your heavenly Father—*your Dad*—who loves you more than you could ever imagine.

Let's talk about that for a second, though. Sometimes dads on earth get too busy to chat, or they have a bad day and don't feel like listening. You probably have even heard of some parents who aren't that great at being parents. Our moms and dads are human. They don't always get it right. But God is different. He's *the perfect parent*, and He's always ready to talk to you.

WHAT TALKING TO GOD CAN DO FOR YOU

- Prayer lets you hand over all your worries and fears to God.
- Prayer reminds you that God is bigger and more powerful than any problem you'll ever face.

Think about how you talk to your dad or granddad. You probably run right up and start talking about all kinds of things. You might say, "Hey, Dad, listen to this!" or "Papa, look what I figured out how to do!" Do you worry about where you are, what time it is, or getting your words just right? Of course not! Well, that's how God wants you to talk to Him too.

I'M AFRAID I'LL MESS UP WHEN I PRAY

You're not alone. Plenty of people are afraid they'll mess up when they talk to God. After all, He's *God!* You have to follow a whole bunch of special rules, right?

Wrong!

There's no one right way to pray. You don't have to worry about getting your

DID YOU KNOW...?

When Jesus was on earth, He sometimes called God by a special name. It was *Abba*, which means "Dad" or "Daddy."

- Prayer helps you stick close to God (kind of like glue but stronger and not as messy).
- Prayer helps you know who God is and how much He loves you.
- Prayer helps you become the person God made you to be.
- Prayer helps you do the things God wants you to do. Even things that seem impossible! (Like forgiving that kid who always uses you as his dodgeball target.)

words mixed up or using big fancy ones that you can't even spell. It doesn't matter if you're standing up, sitting down, or if your eyes accidentally pop open. Prayer isn't a test, and God isn't grading you.

As long as you come to God with an open heart, your prayers sound just right to Him.

SO, WHAT DO I TALK TO GOD ABOUT?

You mean, what on earth do you say to the One who made the whole earth? Well, anything. Seriously. *Anything* at all.

You can talk to God about the fight you had with your best friend, how you wish that zit would disappear, and how you'd love to have your own room. Talk to Him about your day, the things you wonder about, and the things you worry about.

You can tell God things you don't want to tell anyone else. And if you're sad or scared or even angry, that's okay. God can handle it. Nothing you say will shock or surprise Him. And nothing you say will make Him stop loving you. (Just check out the promise of Romans 8:38–39.)

Here's another great fact about prayer: God is never too busy to listen, and He never gets tired of listening. No matter how much you talk or what you say, He is always ready to hear more.

WHAT DOES THE BIBLE SAY?

Find Matthew 18:2–4 in the Bible. Who does Jesus say His followers should be more like?

WHY PRAY?

1, 2, 3 . . . OR MORE?

How many times a day should you pray? That's a good question, but it doesn't have an answer. That's because prayer isn't a chore. There's no list on the refrigerator to check off, such as "clean your room," "brush your teeth," or "feed the dog."

Prayer is a continual conversation. Think about it: Do you count how many times a day you talk to your friends, your parents, or your brothers and sisters? No! You just talk to them whenever you want to or need to.

DON'T FORGET!

Nothing can separate us from the love God has for us.
—Romans 8:38

That's how God wants you to be with Him too. Talk to Him whenever you need to or want to. Chances are, the more you talk to God, the more you'll *want* to talk to Him.

After a while, you might start having a conversation with God *before* you realize you're *actually praying*. And that's great! Those quick conversations help you stay close to God throughout your day. (It's also important to plan a special time each day to pray. But don't worry. We'll talk more about those prayer times later.)

NEVER STOP PRAYING?

God loves it when you pray. He loves it so much that He wants you to pray all the time! In fact, when the church was first getting started, Jesus' followers gathered together and prayed "constantly" (Acts 1:14 NIV). Later the apostle Paul told believers to "never stop praying" (1 Thessalonians 5:17).

PRAY FIRST

TEN TIMES TO PRAY

1. Before you get out of bed
2. Before you brush your teeth
3. Before you eat
4. Before you walk into school
5. Before you step onto the court or field
6. Before you take a test
7. Before you meet your friends
8. Before you do something with your family
9. Before you open the Bible
10. Before you go to sleep

All the time? Constantly? Never stop? How is it even possible to pray like that? You've got classes and practice and family stuff. Life is crazy busy! How can you pray all the time? Here's the answer: Pray as much as you can while you're doing other stuff.

After all, you do two things at once all the time. Like running *and* dribbling a basketball. Eating *and* laughing with your friends. Watching videos *and* doing your homework. Okay, that last one isn't the best example, but you get the idea.

One simple way to do this is to keep God in your thoughts. For example, when you go outside, think about how God made the sky and trees and say, "Thanks!" Or when you meet your friends, think about how good God is to bring them into your life.

Another way is to pray one-sentence prayers as you go throughout your day, such as *God, what do You think about me trying out for the band?* Or *Thanks, God, for a great lunch.* Or *Please help my mom to have a good day at work.*

PRAY FIRST

Remember how we said prayer is a conversation with God? Well, He doesn't want to be the last one you talk to. And although He wants you to hand over all your troubles and problems to Him, God doesn't want to hear from you *only* when you need His help.

God wants to be first in your life. The first One you think of and the first One you turn to. One way to keep Him first is to pray first.

In other words, pray *before* you do something or *before* you need His help. For example, before you get out of bed, pray, "Thank You for a great night of sleep, God." Or before you go over to a friend's house, pray, "Help me to be a good friend today."

REMEMBER . . .

Prayer builds a personal connection—a relationship, a friendship—between you and God. The more you spend time with Him in prayer, the stronger that relationship will be. And that's what God wants most: that you turn to Him and pray first!

God, I'm kind of amazed that You want to talk to me. And incredibly grateful. And, honestly, maybe a little nervous. But I'm starting to understand that prayer isn't about getting the words just right. It's about loving You, trusting You, and getting to know You better. I *do* love and trust You. And I *do* want to know You better. So please help me as I learn more about prayer and talking to You. And, God? Thank You for listening. In Jesus' name, amen.

WHAT DO YOU THINK?

1. Is it easy to talk to God, or do you feel a little nervous? And if you do sometimes feel nervous, what makes you feel that way?

_____

_____

_____

_____

_____

_____

WHY PRAY?

2. Imagine you're explaining prayer to someone who has never heard of it before. How would you describe it in your own words? What are some everyday examples of ways you pray that you could share?

_____

_____

_____

_____

_____

_____

3. How does it make you feel to know that God wants to talk to *you*?

_____

_____

_____

_____

_____

_____

CHAPTER 2

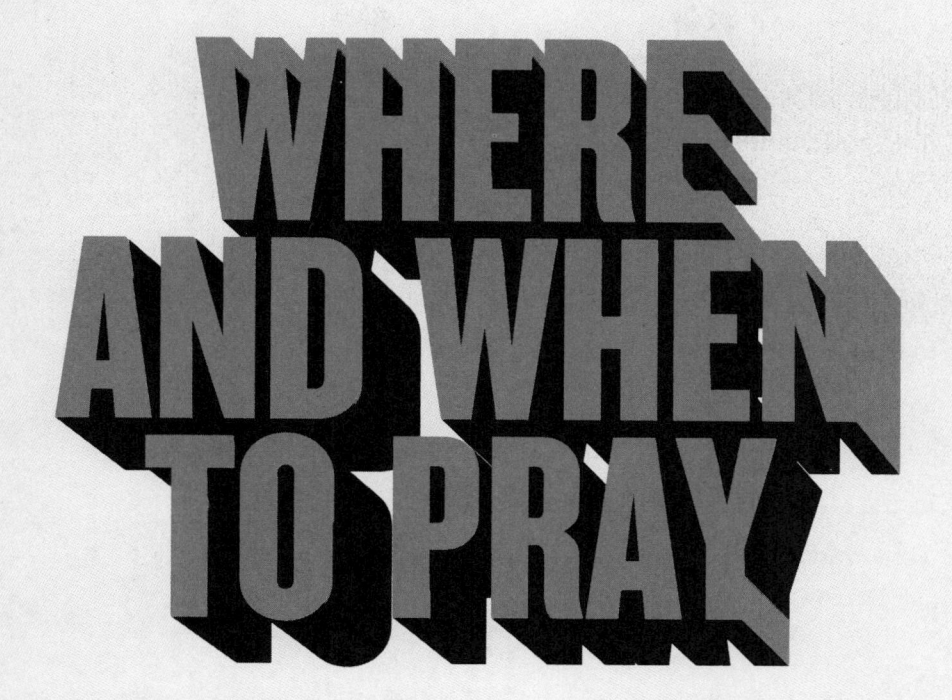

WHERE AND WHEN TO PRAY

ANYTIME AND ANYWHERE... THAT'S WHEN AND WHERE GOD WANTS TO HEAR FROM YOU.

TIME AND PLACE: DOES IT MATTER?

For lots of things in this world, the *when* and *where* are pretty important.

Take basketball, for example. It's a great game to play. But maybe *not* at 3:00 A.M. or in the living room. That could cause problems. The same is true with practicing your trumpet or guitar or xylophone. Plenty of times and places work great for that. But right outside your mom's office while she's working probably isn't one of them.

What about prayer, then? Is the *when* and *where* important when it comes to prayer?

The answer is yes.

And the answer is also no.

YES AND NO?

The fact is, *yes*, God wants to hear from you—and is 100 percent ready to listen to you—no matter where you are or what time it is.

- In the middle of the afternoon at the park? God's listening.
- On the stage in the middle of a rehearsal? He's listening.
- In the middle of the night when everyone else is asleep? Yep. He's listening then too.

God will never ever, ever say to you, *Shhh! Not now. This isn't the right time or place to pray.*

But . . . while it's true that you can talk to God anytime and anywhere, He loves it when you set aside a special time and place to talk to Him—just you and God spending time together.

BIBLE READING TIPS

- Begin with a prayer, like, "Lord, help me to learn from Your Word today."
- Read the verses. Then read them again.
- Think about what the verses mean. What do they tell you about God? What do they tell you about how you should live?

WHERE AND WHEN TO PRAY

AFTER ALL, JESUS DID . . .

Jesus was serious about prayer. Sure, He had lots of conversations with God that sort of happened naturally throughout the day. But He also planned out special times and places to be alone and talk to God. Here's just one example:

> Early the next morning, Jesus woke and left the house while it was still dark. He went to a place to be alone and pray. (Mark 1:35)

Look at all that Jesus did to put His prayer time first: He got up early, went to a special place, and made sure He had time alone. If Jesus did all that, it's probably a good idea for you also.

THE WHEN

So *when* should your special time with God be? That's really up to you. Pick a time of day when you can be alone—without being distracted by other people or stuff—and try to make it the same time every day. Of course, you might have to switch it up every once in a while, but don't do it too often.

Keeping your prayer time at the same time every day will help it become a habit. That will make it easier to remember and easier to do.

- Is there a word or a part of the verse that jumps out at you? Why?
- Not sure where to begin reading your Bible? Pick one of the Gospels—Matthew, Mark, Luke, or John—and read about when Jesus was on earth.

You might like to pray first thing in the morning. (Just make sure you can stay awake!) You might like to slip away after school and before you dive into homework. Or you might like to talk to God before bedtime. Maybe try out a few different times in the beginning to figure out what works best for you.

THE WHERE

Why does the *where* matter? Think about it this way: Do you and your friends have a favorite table in the lunchroom where you always meet? Or maybe a certain spot in the hallways before school or church? If you want to meet up with your friends, then *that* is the place to go, right? In the same way, when you choose a special spot for prayer, it becomes your place to meet with God.

Here's something really cool about having a special spot for prayer: After you've been praying there for a few days, your mind and body will *know* it's the place for praying. So when you go to that spot, your mind and body actually get ready to pray! (It's kind of like when you climb into bed and your mind and body begin to get sleepy.)

CREATE YOUR OWN PRAYER SPOT

PICK THE PLACE: Think of a Prayer Spot where you can be alone with God. Is there somewhere quiet where you won't be interrupted by people walking around or distracted by the TV or other noises? Pick a place where you can talk out loud to God without worrying who might hear you. It should be comfy, but not so comfy that you fall asleep! Your Prayer Spot could be in a closet or a corner of your room. It could be by the window or in a favorite chair. It could even be under a favorite tree or up in a treehouse.

WHERE AND WHEN TO PRAY

HANG IT UP

Write out the words of Psalm 17:6 (or another favorite verse) on a piece of poster board or colorful paper. Add your own decorations and artwork around it. Perhaps even put it in a frame! Hang it up in your Prayer Spot so you'll see it every day.

BUT WHAT DO I DO?

Okay, you've got your Prayer Spot all picked out. You've got your Bible and a comfy place to sit. Now what? What do you *do* in this Prayer Spot?

MAKE IT PERSONAL: Make it your own by adding some of these items:
- A Bible
- Pens and highlighters (the kind made for writing in Bibles are especially awesome)
- Paper or a journal for writing down thoughts and prayers
- A cozy chair or pillows
- A small table or basket to hold your things
- A water bottle (with stickers or without)
- Headphones or a small speaker for worship music

PRAY FIRST

There is only one rule: *Spend time with God.* Exactly how you do that is up to you. But here are some suggestions:

• Listen to God by reading His words in the Bible.

• Write down your thoughts about what you read or any thoughts you have while talking to God.

• Pray. Talk to God. You can talk to Him in your thoughts. You can whisper what you want to say. You can say your prayers out loud or even shout them out—which is especially awesome when you're praising Him and telling Him how awesome He is! (We'll talk more about *what* to pray later in the book.)

• Listen to and sing along with worship songs.

• Simply be still and be with God.

DID YOU KNOW...?

In Jesus' time, Jewish men wore a *tallit* (or prayer shawl) around their shoulders or around their cloaks. When they wanted to pray but couldn't be alone, they pulled this cloth up over their heads. It was like their own private tent to shut out the world so they could talk to God.

HOW LONG?

The question you might ask next is: *How long should I talk to God?*

You can talk to Him for a few minutes, an hour, or more! But chances are, in the beginning, this might take a little getting used to. That's okay! Think about how long it took you to really get comfortable talking about personal stuff to your best friend.

WHERE AND WHEN TO PRAY

The more time you spend alone with God, the easier it will get. Try starting out with five minutes and build up to ten. After that, try fifteen and then more. Before you know it, you'll be so caught up in talking to God that you won't even know what time it is.

> **TALLIT (TALL-EET):** a woven cloth or shawl that is held over the head of someone who wants to pray in private

A TALLIT FOR YOU?

You might not want to wear a tallit around school or to ball practice, but you can create a private space for yourself even when you're in a busy place. Step away as much as you can, close your eyes (if you can), put in your earbuds—if you have them—and play some soft worship music. If you are wearing a hoodie, pull up the hood. Then simply talk to God.

GO TO YOUR ROOM

No, you're not in trouble! "Go to your room" is how Jesus told His followers to pray in Matthew 6:5–6. Jesus wanted them to understand that prayer should be private and personal. It's between you and God.

Does that mean you should never pray in public? Nope, absolutely not! Then why

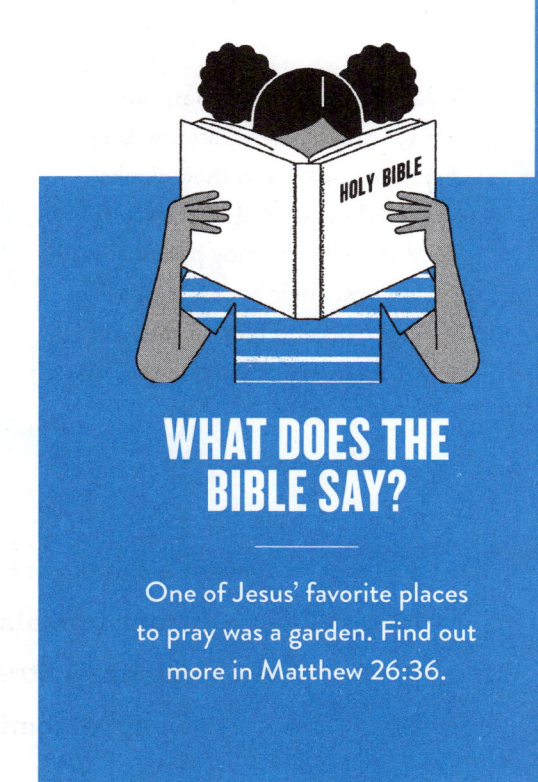

> **WHAT DOES THE BIBLE SAY?**
>
> One of Jesus' favorite places to pray was a garden. Find out more in Matthew 26:36.

PRAY FIRST

> **TAMEION (TAM-I-ON):** the Greek word for room or closet. This was a storage room or secret room in many Jewish homes during the time of Jesus. It was used for storing food and linens and for hiding valuables and money. So it makes sense that Jesus would say to take your treasure of prayer into this kind of room!

did Jesus say that? Because some people were praying for the wrong reasons. They were more interested in showing off how good and "holy" they were than in actually talking to God.

Prayer isn't about who sees you or how many fancy words you use. It's about talking to God, worshiping Him, and getting to know Him better. Prayer is a treasure. You don't have to hide it, but remember to treat it as a priceless gift.

MIX IT UP

Having a Prayer Spot helps you remember to make prayer a priority. At least until the Prayer Spot stops helping. If you start to get bored, or if praying in that place or at that time becomes a struggle, mix it up and change your routine. Try these ideas:

- Find or create a different spot.
- Try a different time.
- Add some music or take it away.
- Turn the lights off or on.

Remember, there's no right or wrong place to pray. The important thing is to pray!

WHERE AND WHEN TO PRAY

TAKE IT OUTSIDE

One of the best places to talk to God is outside in the amazing world He created. Maybe that's because it's never the same place twice. Leaves change colors, birds come and go, clouds move, and the weather is different every day. Almost every time Jesus prayed in the Bible, it was outside in His Father's world!

REMEMBER . . .

God isn't picky about the when or the where. He just wants you to pray!

> God, I'm still amazed that You want to talk to me every single day. Help me find the time and place that work best for me. I want to make prayer a habit. But more than that, God, I want a stronger desire to talk to You every day. And I can't wait to get to know You better! In Jesus' name, amen.

WHAT DO YOU THINK?

1. Think of three different Prayer Spots you could use, and try them out. Which one works best for you? Why?

   _____
   _____
   _____
   _____

2. Step outside and talk to God in His creation today. How is praying outside different from praying inside?

   _____
   _____
   _____
   _____
   _____

CHAPTER 3
WHAT TO PRAY

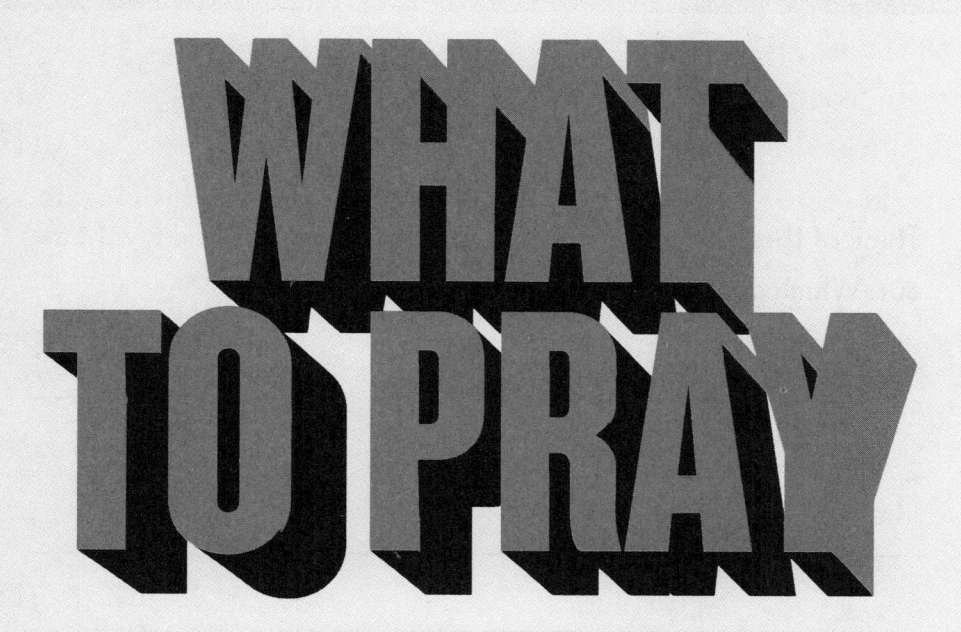

WHEN YOU'RE NOT SURE WHAT TO PRAY, ASK GOD. HE'LL HELP YOU FIGURE OUT WHAT TO SAY.

YOU NEED A PLAN

If you want to be serious about prayer, you need a plan for what to pray about.

Now, maybe you're thinking, *But I thought I could talk to God anytime, anywhere, and about anything. Why do I need a plan?*

Because a plan will help you make the most of your prayer time and have a great conversation with God. Without a plan, it's easy to end up talking about whatever pops into your head—and that's okay. Sometimes. But when it comes to your special prayer time, you should be a bit more serious about what you say. And for that, you need a plan.

IS THIS WEIRD?

Does planning your prayers still feel a little weird?

Try thinking of it this way: Imagine that you and a bunch of your friends are meeting to plan a party. This is the only chance you have to meet, and you only have a short time to get everything figured out. You have so much to talk about, like . . .

- Where will the party be?
- When will it start?
- Who will you invite?
- What kind of food will you have?
- Who will bring the food?
- Will there be music?
- Will you play games?

If you want to get all that figured out in one meeting, you need a plan to make the most of your time together.

It's the same with God. You need a plan to make the most of your special prayer time with Him.

ATTITUDE, ATTITUDE

The first step in your plan is all about having the right attitude. Here's why: Have you ever gotten in trouble because of your attitude? Maybe your mouth says the right words, like, "Okay. I'll do it, Dad." But the tone of your voice and the look on your face "say" you don't like it one bit.

Attitude is just as important as the words you say. Especially when you're

HELLO, GOD

If you're wondering how to start out your prayers with a good attitude, take a look at these examples.

- Dear God . . .
- Good morning, Lord.
- Thank You, God, for this amazing day.
- Hi, God. It's me.
- God, I'm so grateful that You are always ready to listen.

What would you add?

talking to God. He wants to know that He's important to you and that you really do want to talk to Him.

Imagine what would happen if you barged in after school, slammed the door against the wall, and yelled, "Hey, Mom, I need some money for a field trip!" How rude, right? Your mom would be much happier if you said hello, gave her a hug, and asked about her day *before* telling her what you want or need.

In the same way, you don't want to barge right into prayer with God and start asking Him to give you things.

NOT THE DRIVE-THRU

God isn't like a drive-thru. You shouldn't just jump in with a list of stuff you want like, "Hey, God, I'd like to score a major goal in the game tomorrow with a side of great times with my friends. Oh, and could You add an A on my math test to that?"

God is your Abba Father, and He loves you more than anything. He wants to give you good things. But most of all, He wants to give you a relationship

PRAY FIRST

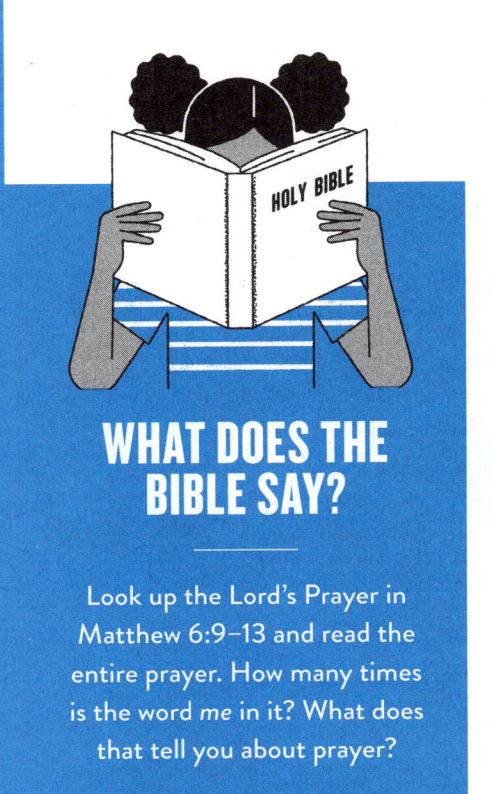

with Him, and that's something you will build together. So yeah, definitely ask God for all those things you want. Definitely do that. But also make sure your prayers let God know that *you know* who He is—the Lord of all creation. Your words should tell Him that you love Him for who He is—not what He can give you.

WHAT DO I SAY?

Has this ever happened to you? You're in class, and the teacher is asking questions. You did the homework, so you know the answers. But when it's your turn to answer a question, you suddenly can't think of a thing to say!

We've all faced a situation like that, right? But what do class questions have to do with prayer?

WHAT DOES THE BIBLE SAY?

Look up the Lord's Prayer in Matthew 6:9–13 and read the entire prayer. How many times is the word *me* in it? What does that tell you about prayer?

The point is, there will be times when you don't know what to pray.

It's okay. You're learning. Jesus' disciples didn't always know what to pray either. Of course, they *did* have Jesus right there with them—the ultimate expert on prayer—so they could ask Him. Which they did. And He told them. Jesus' answer is written in the Bible, so we can know the answer too. Let's check it out.

THE LORD'S PRAYER

The prayer Jesus gave His disciples is called the Lord's Prayer. And it really is a great prayer to memorize.

But here's the thing: When Jesus gave His disciples this prayer, it wasn't so they could memorize it and repeat it back to God. And it wasn't so you could memorize it and repeat it back to God either.

Instead, Jesus taught His disciples—and you—*how* to pray. Each line of the prayer is like a tool to help you remember the kinds of things you need and want to talk to God about.

Because prayer shouldn't be like a speech you memorize for school. Prayer should help you grow closer to God and get to know Him better.

WHO'S THAT YOU'RE TALKING TO?

The whole purpose of prayer is to connect with God. That's exactly what Jesus did with the very first words of the Lord's Prayer:

"Our Father in heaven" (Matthew 6:9)

Jesus started by calling out to His Father. His words were warm and personal because He was talking to His Dad. It's kind of like walking into your house and calling out, "Hey, Dad!"

DID YOU KNOW...?

In Jesus' time, the Jewish people memorized many prayers. They said certain prayers on certain days, at certain times, and for certain celebrations. One of these prayers was called the Shema (shuh-MAH), and the ancient Jews prayed these words every morning and evening:

*Hear, O Israel: The L*ORD *our God, the L*ORD *is one. Love the L*ORD *your God with all your heart and with all your soul and with all your strength.* (Deuteronomy 6:4–5 NIV)

Jesus invites you to start your prayers the same way—calling out to your perfect heavenly Dad.

So yes, memorize the Lord's Prayer. But instead of just repeating it back to God, use it to help you plan out what to pray. We'll really dive into this in chapter 6. But for now, hold on to this truth: It's more than a perfect prayer—it's a perfect plan for your prayers.

IT'S NOT A SHOW, AND THERE ARE NO BONUS POINTS

When Jesus was on earth, some people made a habit of praying for all the wrong reasons. They prayed loud, long prayers in the marketplaces and on the street corners where everyone could see them. They were really good at it too. They knew all the big fancy words, and they used lots of them. However, these people weren't really talking to God. They were putting on a show.

Jesus warned His disciples against these "show-off prayers":

> "When you pray, don't be like the hypocrites. They love to stand in the synagogues and on the street corners and pray loudly. They want people to see them pray. I tell you the truth. They already have their full reward." (Matthew 6:5)

Other people thought that if they said more words, God would answer their prayers more. They repeated the same words over and over again. Jesus warned about this too:

> "Don't be like those people who don't know God. They continue saying things that mean nothing. They think that God will hear them because of the many things they say." (Matthew 6:7)

WHAT TO PRAY

Prayer isn't a show, and you don't get bonus points for extra words. Prayer is a personal, private conversation between you and God.

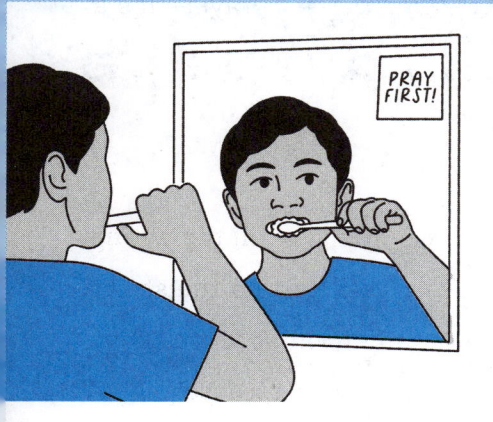

LINK IT UP

You definitely want to plan out your special prayer time with God. But you can also make a plan to pray throughout the day. A great way to do this is to link (or connect) prayer to something you do every day. For example, when you brush your teeth, ask God to help all the words that come out of your mouth today to be good and helpful. What are some other things you do every day? How could you use those times to remind you to pray? Take notes in the margins so you don't forget!

EVERY PLAN HAS A PURPOSE

Plans are made for a reason. They have a purpose—to make something happen. For example, the purpose of a treehouse plan is to build a treehouse, and the purpose of a homework plan is to get better grades. In the same way, the purpose of the Lord's Prayer is to help you grow closer to God. Which is an awesome plan!

REMEMBER . . .

Don't just pray first—plan what to pray first!

Abba Father, I want to start my prayer like Jesus did—by calling out to You as my Father. Because that is who You are, my perfect Father in heaven. I know You created this world and everything in it, including me. But, God, I want to know even more about You. Please teach me something new about You today. Thank You, Father. In Jesus' name, amen.

WHAT DO YOU THINK?

1. How could a plan for your prayers—how you talk to God and what you talk to Him about—help you grow closer to God?

_____

_____

_____

_____

_____

_____

_____

_____

WHAT TO PRAY

2. As you work out a plan for your prayers, think about why you are praying. Is it to show off or to get what you want? Or is it to grow closer to God?

_____

_____

_____

_____

_____

3. Think of five things you do every day. Write out a one-sentence prayer to say before you do each of those things.

_____

_____

_____

_____

_____

CHAPTER 4

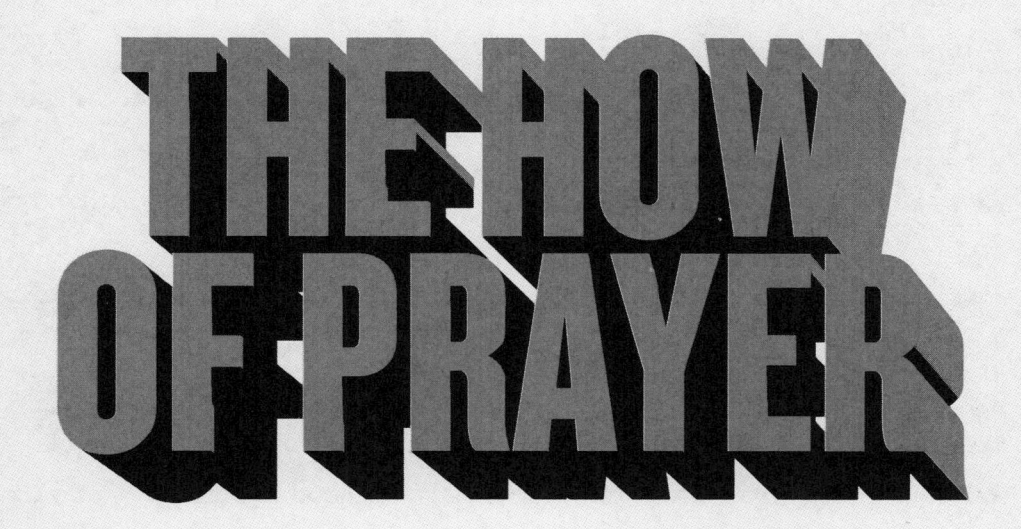

THE HOW OF PRAYER

WHEN YOU PRAY, GREAT THINGS HAPPEN, AND THEY START IN YOUR OWN HEART.

MAKE A DIFFERENCE

Have you ever wanted to make a difference in the world? To make it a better place? You can! Though the *way* you change the world might surprise you. Sure, you can do and say things that are good and helpful. But if you want to really make a difference, pray.

Yes, pray! Because when you pray, you tap into the power of God—and there is nothing He can't do.

Got troubles at school? Pray.

Want to have a better, safer neighborhood? Pray.

PRAY FIRST

Worried about someone you love? Pray.

Not sure what to do? Pray.

Think you know what to do? Pray.

Prayer can do what nothing else will do. And it will work when nothing else will. So if you want to change the world—or at least your corner of it—then pray! Because when you pray, you're asking God to use *His power* to make a difference.

PRAYER WALK

Take a walk. Not just any old walk, but a *Prayer Walk*. Grab some friends or your family and take a walk around your neighborhood or town. As you walk, pray about the homes and businesses you pass by. Pray for the people who live and work there. And pray that God will show you who and how you can help. Try a Prayer Walk through the hallways of your school and around your church too.

PRAYER WALK PRAYERS

Are you wondering what to pray on your Prayer Walk? Here are a few examples to get you started.

- Lord, shine Your light and love into our neighborhood. Chase away all the darkness of crime and hate.
- Please keep everyone here on our street safe.
- God, please show me how to be a good neighbor.

THE SECRET TO POWERFUL PRAYER

There's a secret when it comes to powerful prayers. Okay, it's not really a secret because God tells us in the Bible over and over again what it is. The power isn't in the words you say, where you pray, or whether you close your eyes to pray. The power is in who you're praying to: God!

Because the most powerful force on earth isn't an army or any of its weapons. It's not Space Force. The most powerful force on earth is God's power when He answers the prayers of His people. Nothing is impossible for Him!

A STORY ABOUT PRAYER

One day after Jesus had returned to heaven, His disciples Peter and John went to the temple. On the way, they met a beggar who had been crippled his whole life and couldn't work. When Peter and John passed by, he begged them for money.

Peter said, "I don't have any silver or gold, but I do have something else I can give you: By the power of Jesus Christ from Nazareth—stand up and walk!" (Acts 3:6).

- Father, be with each person here—the students, teachers, and staff. Help us to be kind to one another.
- God, when my friends and I run into a bully, help us to know what to do.
- God, please show me someone I can talk to about Jesus—and help me to have the courage to do it.
- Lord, please guide our leaders. Help them to make good decisions.
- Please open the hearts of my neighbors to want to know more about You.

PRAY FIRST

And the man did! He jumped up and began walking and praising God. People gathered around. They knew this man had been crippled his whole life. How was he walking and even jumping now?

While everyone watched the man jump around, Peter and John taught about Jesus. They preached for hours, and more than five thousand people believed! But the religious and political leaders didn't like that at all. What they did like was having power over the people. They were afraid they would lose that power if people started following Jesus. So they arrested Peter and John and threw them in prison!

DID YOU KNOW...?

The Sanhedrin was like a supreme court for the ancient Jews. It made the final decisions about the religious laws. Unfortunately, the leaders loved their power more than they loved God. They also put Jesus on trial after He was arrested—and found Him guilty!

The next day, Peter and John appeared before the leaders in the Sanhedrin—and Peter and John told them about Jesus. But the Jewish leaders didn't believe. In fact, they told Peter and John to stop preaching about Jesus—or else. Then they sent Peter and John home.

Peter and John went to the other believers and told them what happened. They all gathered to pray. Can you guess what they prayed? Did they pray for safety? Did they ask God to never send them to prison again?

"Help us to speak your word without fear" (Acts 4:29). *That* was their prayer. Pretty amazing, right?

THE HOW OF PRAYER

Well, God's answer was even more amazing. The place where they were meeting shook, the Holy Spirit filled every person, and they spoke boldly about Jesus without any fear (Acts 4:31)!

This true story about Peter and John tells us three things about powerful prayers:

1. They are prayed together with other believers.
2. They are based on the Bible.
3. They are bold!

PRAY TOGETHER!

When Peter and John told the other believers what happened, they "raised their voices together in prayer" (Acts 4:24 NIV). They didn't wait for Peter and John to lead them. They didn't have one person pray while everyone else listened and nodded their heads. They didn't do a prayer circle or whisper to themselves. No, they raised their voices in prayer!

Powerful prayers are the prayers we pray together. They're *unified*.

Now, a lot of crazy stuff is going on in the world, right? People are looking for answers and ways to fix problems. But God is the only One who can make the world better. We'll start to get the answer the world needs when we come together and pray together. Just check out this promise:

> If my people, who are called by my name, will humble themselves and pray and seek my face and turn from their wicked ways, then I will hear from heaven, and I will forgive their sin and will heal their land. (2 Chronicles 7:14 NIV)

UNIFIED (YU-NIH-FIED): to be brought together as one

PRAYER POWER!

Is there something in your neighborhood, your school, your church, or the world that needs to change? Gather a group of family or friends and pray together about it. And not just once. Agree to meet once a month or once a week to pray together. You can even set a time when you will all stop and pray every day. For example, maybe everyone stops at 8:00 P.M. for a moment and prays for your school. You might not be together in person, but your hearts will be together in God.

Do this for at least fourteen days and pay attention to the changes. They may be small at first, but God is already working. Keep praying! What changes do you see after thirty days? After fifty? After one hundred days? After six months or a year?

Remember, some of the greatest changes may not be visible. In fact, some of the greatest changes will happen in your heart.

PRAY THE PROMISES

Did you know that you can pray God's promises? Straight out of the Bible. That's right, you can pray God's Word right back to Him.

There are about four thousand promises of God in the Bible. And every single one was fulfilled by Jesus (2 Corinthians 1:20). You might not see them all yet, but God's "Yes!" to those promises is coming.

So when you pray God's promises back to Him, you are saying that you believe He will keep them. And believing that He will keep His promises builds your house on the rock.

Wait . . . what? What rock? And where did the house come from? Keep reading!

On the Rock

Jesus said, "Everyone who hears these things I say and obeys them is like a wise man. The wise man built his house on rock" (Matthew 7:24). Do you remember that story about the wise man? He built his house on the rock, and no storm could knock it down. Unlike the other guy in Jesus' story, who built his house on the sand. When the storms came, that house went SPLAT!

When you believe God's promises, you are like that wise man. Your life and prayers will be built on the rock of His Word. So whenever a problem, trouble, or worry comes your way, trust God and find a promise to pray—and avoid that whole SPLAT! thing!

But Be Careful

Praying a promise isn't a game, and it definitely isn't a spell. The power doesn't come from you or the words you say. You can't make whatever you want happen.

This is what happens instead: When you pray God's Word back to Him, you are declaring that you trust Him. That you believe He will do what He has promised.

> **DON'T FORGET!**
>
> "For people this is impossible. But for God all things are possible."
> —Mark 10:27

HOW TO PRAY A PROMISE

If you're wondering *how* to pray the promises, here's an example of how to turn a promise into a prayer.

James 1:5 promises, "If any of you needs wisdom, you should ask God for it. God is generous. He enjoys giving to all people, so God will give you wisdom."

You make that promise a prayer by saying something like this: "Lord, I don't know what to do. But Your Word promises that You will help me be wise and make good choices. So please show me the right thing to do. I know You already have the perfect answer for me. In Jesus' name, amen."

You're choosing to focus on God and His power to work in your life—rather than focusing on the problem. It's kind of like saying, "Lord, I'm not sure what to do here, but I know You've got this!"

DON'T BE WIMPY

"Okay, Lord, whatever You want, Your will be done. If You can help me to say no to this temptation, that'd be good."

Do you see anything wrong with this prayer? It's so wimpy! Just look at those words . . . *Whatever? If You can? That'd be good?*

You get to talk to the God who's in charge of oceans, shooting stars, and the ground you're standing on! His power is unlimited, and His promises are rock solid. There's no *"if You can"* with God! If He's made a promise, He will keep it!

Be Bold!

Yes! It's okay to pray boldly. In fact, God loves it when your prayers are bold. Why? Because when you claim one of God's promises in prayer, you are actually praising Him. How? Because you're saying, "God, I *know* You can do this!"

So be bold, praise God, and try a prayer like this: "God, You promised to help me say no to things that are wrong, and I know You'll keep that promise. Please give me the words to say no to this wrong thing. And thanks for helping me say yes to what is right!"

Don't Make the Devil Happy

Wimpy prayers make the devil happy, and who wants that? It's like saying you aren't sure God has the power to answer. And if you can answer your prayer without any help from God, that's like saying you don't need Him or His power in your life.

God wants you to ask for the big things, the bold things—like Peter and John asking for the courage to keep preaching about Jesus when they were threatened with prison or worse.

But what if you aren't sure how God can fix a situation? Then try a prayer like this: "Lord, I don't see a way out of this. But You know everything, and You can do anything. So I'm going to trust You and watch to see what amazing thing You do!"

God loves bold prayers because bold prayers show that you love and trust God.

DID YOU KNOW...?

In James 5:16, the word used to describe prayer comes from the Greek word *energeo* (en-erg-EH-o).[1] Does that look a little familiar? Like *energy*. The kind of energy that *energeo* describes is red-hot, on fire, and boiling over! That's how bold God wants you to be in your prayers. Because that's how bold His power is!

5 PROMISES TO PRAY

1. When you're frightened and need to feel safe: "The LORD will watch over your coming and going both now and forevermore" (Psalm 121:8 NIV).
2. When you need someone to talk to: "God listens to us every time we ask him" (1 John 5:15).
3. When you're tired: "Come to me, all of you who are tired and have heavy loads. I will give you rest" (Matthew 11:28).
4. When you need courage: "Be strong and courageous. Do not be afraid or terrified because of them, for the LORD your God goes with you; he will never leave you nor forsake you" (Deuteronomy 31:6 NIV).
5. When you mess up and sin: "But if we confess our sins, he will forgive our sins. We can trust God. He does what is right. He will make us clean from all the wrongs we have done" (1 John 1:9).

AND A BONUS:

When you're trapped in the maze of the most epic video game you've ever played: "If you go the wrong way—to the right or to the left—you will hear a voice behind you. It will say, 'This is the right way. You should go this way'" (Isaiah 30:21). Okay, maybe that's not what that verse is talking about.

REMEMBER . . .

You can count on God and trust Him to do things you can't do on your own. To really unleash His power, pray together, pray the promises, and pray with boldness.

And above all, pray first!

Lord, I'm sorry for the times I've been wimpy with my prayers. I want to be bold! Open my eyes to see the things that You want me to pray about—the things in my school, neighborhood, and life. I can't wait to see what You show me! In Jesus' name, amen.

WHAT DO YOU THINK?

1. Think of one of your favorite promises from God. (You can choose one from the list in this chapter or another one you love.) How can you turn it into a prayer?

_____

_____

_____

_____

_____

_____

_____

2. Why would a wimpy prayer be insulting to God? How could you turn a wimpy prayer into a bold one?

_____
_____
_____
_____
_____

3. Mark 10:27 says that "for God all things are possible." What seems impossible in your life right now? Write out a prayer—a bold prayer!—asking God to do the impossible.

_____
_____
_____
_____
_____

CHAPTER 5

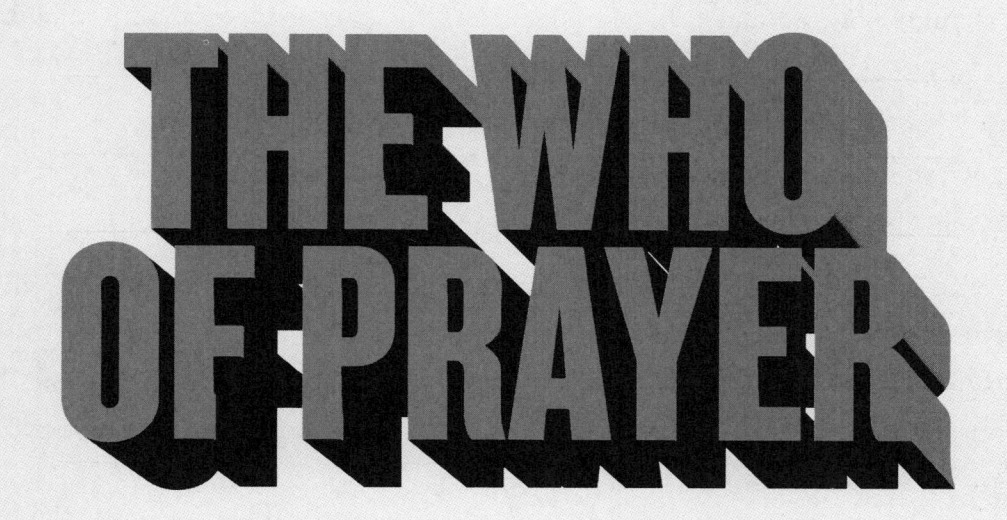

THE WHO OF PRAYER

WHEN YOU PRAY, THE GOD OF THE UNIVERSE LEANS DOWN TO LISTEN TO YOU.

IT'S ALL ABOUT RELATIONSHIP

How many kinds of relationships do you have? Are they all the same? Of course not!

Your relationship with a friend is much different than your relationship with your mom or dad, right? And your relationship with a parent is going to look a lot different than the relationship you have with a teacher or coach.

Each of those people adds something to your life, though. It might be laughter and encouragement, love and support, or wisdom and guidance. Different relationships play different roles in your life.

SOMETHING SPECIAL ABOUT GOD

When it comes to relationships, there's something extra special about God that you should know. Actually, there are lots of extra-special things about God, but let's talk about this one.

God is not just one person. He's three persons in one.

Read that again.

What?! It's a little hard to wrap your head around, right? God is actually God the Father, God the Son, and God the Holy Spirit. All in one. Sometimes these three persons of God are called the *Trinity* or the *Godhead*.

How is that possible? Well, some people compare the Trinity to an egg. (It sounds crazy, but hang on.) An egg has a shell, a yolk, and the egg white, right? Those are three different parts but still one egg.

Others compare the Trinity to water because it can be either ice, liquid, or steam depending on how hot or cold it is. But all three forms are still water.

> **TRINITY (TRIH-NUH-TEE):** The three persons who make up the one God. The three persons are God the Father, God the Son, and God the Holy Spirit.

Honestly, these examples don't fully explain the Trinity, and it's impossible to completely understand God because He's . . . well, He's God! But you can learn more about Him and how the three persons of the Trinity help you pray.

EACH A LITTLE DIFFERENT

Prayer is all about having a personal relationship with God, which means that you need to know who He is. *All three persons of Him.* (It's still a little hard to understand, isn't it? Don't worry. Nobody has it completely figured out. But one day, you'll understand when you meet Him face-to-face. Or is it face-to-Face-to-Face-to-Face?)

THE WHO OF PRAYER

Each person of the Trinity is special and does something a little different. Paul explained it best in this blessing from 2 Corinthians 13:14: "The grace of the Lord Jesus Christ, the love of God, and the fellowship of the Holy Spirit be with you all."

- The grace of Jesus
- The love of God
- The fellowship of the Holy Spirit

Let's dive in and see what that is all about.

THE AMAZING GRACE OF JESUS

Paul put Jesus first on his list, and it wasn't an accident. Here's why:

1. Jesus is the Mediator between you and God, and He is also your Intercessor.
2. It's because of Jesus that you can be part of God's family.

Because of Jesus

You've probably noticed that people usually end prayers with "in Jesus' name." There's a reason for that. When Jesus came to earth, died on the cross, and rose again, He became our *Mediator*. He opened up the way for us to be in the presence of God. He died to make that connection for us.

Before Jesus, sin got in the way. It created a kind of wall between people and God. Before Jesus, the Jews had all kinds of rules about prayer. And some things

> **MEDIATOR (MEE-DEE-A-TER):** someone who works to bring peace between two opposing sides

47

WHAT DOES THE BIBLE SAY?

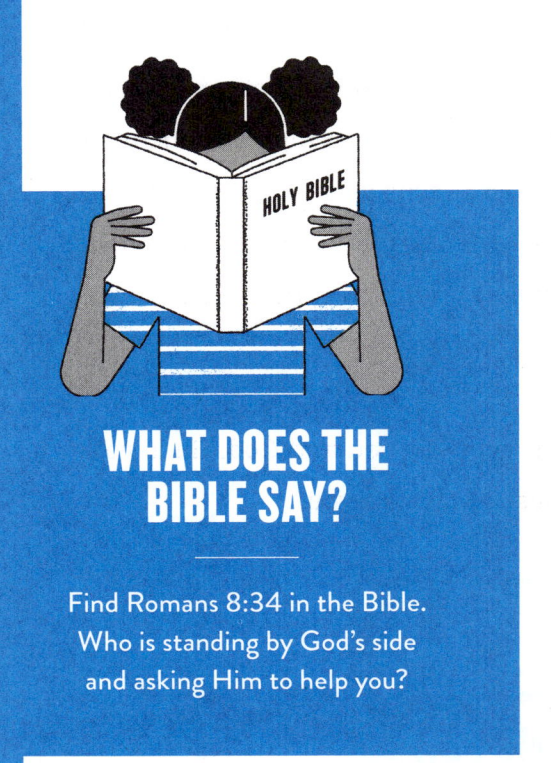

Find Romans 8:34 in the Bible. Who is standing by God's side and asking Him to help you?

could only be done by the priests, who had even more rules to follow. But when Jesus paid the price on the cross for our sins, He broke down that wall between us and God. Because of Jesus, we can talk to God anytime and anywhere.

Talk about amazing grace, right? And it gets even better! Check this out:

You have been saved by grace because you believe. You did not save yourselves. It was a gift from God. (Ephesians 2:8–9)

Did you catch that? When you choose to love and follow Jesus, His grace is a gift—completely free!

Only Jesus

Jesus is the only person of the Trinity to live on earth as a human being. He knows firsthand how tough it can be. Hebrews 4:15–16 says it this way:

For our high priest [Jesus] is able to understand our weaknesses. He was tempted in every way that we are, but he did not sin. Let us, then, feel free to come before God's throne. Here there is grace. And we can receive mercy and grace to help us when we need it.

Think about that for a second. Jesus was tempted to do wrong in every way that you're tempted to do wrong. That means He got mad at His brothers and sisters. He didn't always want to obey Mary and Joseph. He was tempted to show off. Every wrong thing you've ever been tempted to do, Jesus was tempted to do too. But He didn't do any of them. He always chose to do the right thing (because He's perfect). He understands, though, how hard it is to do the right thing sometimes.

Even More Amazing

Jesus does more than create a connection between you and God. He is your *Intercessor*. That's a fancy way of saying that Jesus prays for you.

LOOK WHO'S PRAYING FOR YOU!

The next time you say a prayer, imagine Jesus turning to God the Father and explaining what you need and why you need it. Maybe He says something like this: "Dad, I'm here for _____.
[Insert your name.]

They're having a hard time right now. I know it's hard because I went through the same thing. _____ really needs our help right now!"
[Insert your name.]

How awesome is that?

A PICTURE OF PRAYER

Just as Jesus prays for you, you can be an intercessor and pray for others too. Think of the people and situations in your life that could use a little extra help from God right now and say a prayer for them.

To help you remember, gather (or draw) pictures of the people and things you want to pray for. Cut them out and glue them onto a piece of heavy paper. Put it in your Prayer Spot so you'll see it each time you get ready to pray.

And here's something uber cool: When you pray for others, Jesus prays for them too. It's like an intercessor x 2!

THE LOVE OF GOD THE FATHER

Think of someone who loves you a whole lot. It feels pretty awesome to be loved like that, doesn't it? Well, multiply that love by about a zillion, and you'll get just a glimpse of how much God loves you.

God's love for you is so huge that He wants you with Him forever. That's why He sent His only Son to pay for your sins and completely forgive you. You could never earn that kind of forgiveness on your own. God knew that and made a way for you.

Even more amazing is that when you choose to love and follow God, He adopts you into His family (John 1:12). Jesus becomes your Brother, and God becomes your Father. He even calls you His (Isaiah 43:1). And unlike earthly dads who make mistakes sometimes, God is perfect. His love is perfect. And His care for you is . . . you guessed it . . . perfect.

Fear and Worship

If you read the Old Testament much, you'll soon see all kinds of verses about *fearing* God. Sounds kind of scary, right? (Don't worry. It's not.)

When the Bible talks about fearing the Lord, it isn't referring to a terrified, hiding-under-the-covers kind of fear. And it isn't an "I'm in big trouble now" kind of fear either. Instead, this kind of fear is about worship and respect and awe. It's like coming to God and saying, "Wow! You are awesome!"

So the next time you see the words *fear the Lord*, think of it as "worship the Lord" instead.

A LOST SON AND AN AWESOME DAD

Have you heard the story of the lost son? It's a story Jesus told in Luke 15:11–32 about a father whose younger son made some bad choices. It started when that younger son went up to his father one day and basically said, "I want my inheritance now!"

Rude, right?

But his father still gave him the money. The son took it and ran off to a faraway land where he bought whatever he wanted, did whatever he wanted, and

DID YOU KNOW...?

In the Old Testament, the people had to make a sacrifice on the altar before they could enter the tabernacle. That sacrifice cleansed them from their sins—for a little while—so they could go in and worship God. But when Jesus died on the cross, His sacrifice covered all sins for all time for those who believe in Him. Now, anyone can talk to and worship God. Because of Jesus, nothing can separate us from Him!

PRAY FIRST

hung out with whoever he wanted. Soon, all his money was gone—and then all his friends were gone too. Alone and starving, he ended up feeding pigs to survive. That's when he realized that even the lowest of his father's servants had a better life than he did. The son decided to go home and beg his father to let him be a servant.

Now, his dad could have told the son to get lost. Or he could have said, "You can stay here and work as a servant." But his father did neither. Look at what he did instead:

"While the son was still a long way off, his father saw him coming. He felt sorry for his son. So the father ran to him, and hugged and kissed him." (Luke 15:20)

And that's not all! The father dressed him up in new clothes, put a ring on his finger, and threw him a huge party!

Making Mistakes

Guess what? God is like the father in that story!

Here's why that's so important: You're going to mess up and make a mistake. You're going to make bad choices and sin. It might be on purpose, like that lost son. Or it might be an accident, like saying a bad word when you didn't mean to.

Some people think that God is just watching and waiting for them to mess up.

> **DON'T FORGET!**
>
> For God so loved the world that he gave his one and only Son, that whoever believes in him shall not perish but have eternal life.
> —John 3:16 NIV

THE WHO OF PRAYER

Then, when they do, He swoops down to punish them. *That's not who God is! And that's not what God does!*

Like the father in that story, God is watching and waiting for you to come to Him. When you do, and when you tell Him how sorry you are for the mistakes you've made, God runs to you and swoops you up in His arms in a great big hug. (Okay, just so you know, chances are that you probably won't *see* God running up to you—though He could if He wanted to! But even if you don't see Him with your eyes, He'll be there to love and forgive you.)

THE FELLOWSHIP OF THE HOLY SPIRIT

Fellowship is a lot like friendship, and that's the role of the third person of the Trinity—God the Holy Spirit. You probably haven't heard as much about Him as you have God and Jesus. Maybe that's because He's called the Spirit and that makes some people freak out and think of things like ghosts.

But you don't have to be afraid of the Holy Spirit. In fact, He's one of the best gifts you'll ever receive. You see, when you become a follower of Jesus, the Holy Spirit is God's gift to You. He comes to live inside you. Did you get that? The Holy Spirit of God comes to live *inside you*! Which means that God is with you *all. the. time.* Everywhere you go, He goes. It's like being with your best friend all day every day.

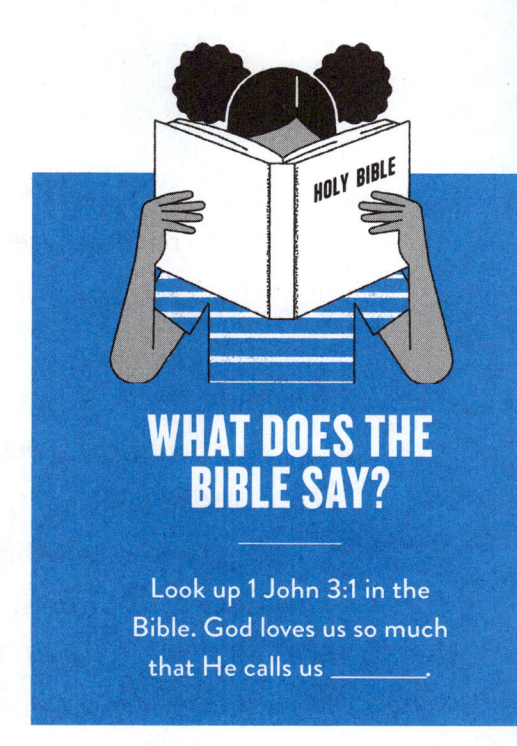

WHAT DOES THE BIBLE SAY?

Look up 1 John 3:1 in the Bible. God loves us so much that He calls us _____.

WHAT DOES THE BIBLE SAY?

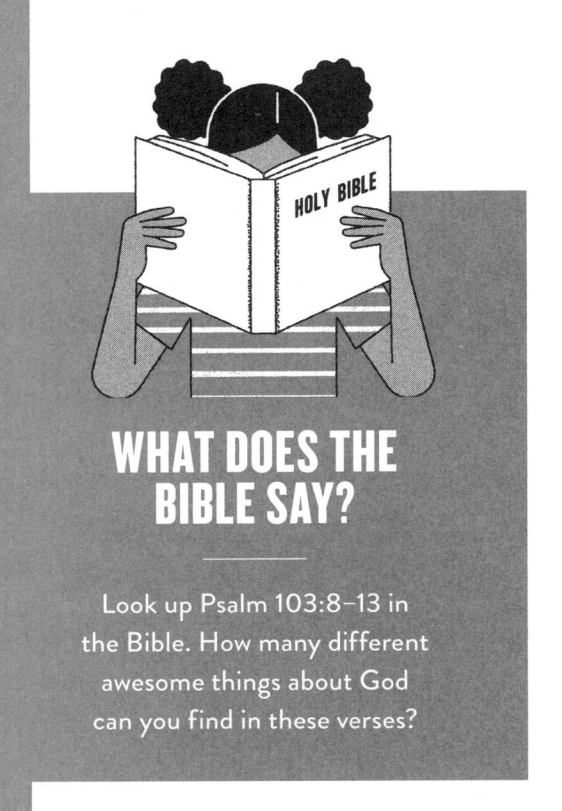

Look up Psalm 103:8–13 in the Bible. How many different awesome things about God can you find in these verses?

The Holy Spirit is a Friend you definitely want to get to know better because He will help you know God and Jesus better. He'll help you live the best possible life—the life God planned for you right from the beginning. You'll recognize Him because He'll be the One whispering in your thoughts, *Okay, let's go! You've got this—just trust Me and remember I'm right here with you every step of the way.*

THREE PERSONS, ONE GOD

God the Father, God the Son, and God the Holy Spirit—they're three different persons, yet they are one God. And you can have a personal relationship with each one of them.

WHAT THE HOLY SPIRIT DOES

The Holy Spirit is incredibly busy in your life. He fills many roles:

- Friend
- Encourager
- Champion

- Guardian
- Teacher
- Comforter

THE WHO OF PRAYER

Worship God the Father, and soak up His great, big, gigantic love.

Believe in and accept the grace of Jesus the Son so you can become a part of God's family and talk to Him in prayer.

And be led by the Holy Spirit, who comes to live inside you so God—and His wisdom, power, and love—is with you every second of every day.

REMEMBER...

Pray first—to God, through the grace of Jesus, and with the help of the Holy Spirit.

DID YOU KNOW...?

The original Greek word for "Holy Spirit" is *parakletos* (par-AK-lay-tos), which means "one who is called to one's side."[1] And that's exactly what the Holy Spirit does—stick right by your side, on the inside!

The Holy Spirit will be a help to you in so many ways:

- He will help you remember all you've learned about God and Jesus (John 14:26).
- He will give you strength when you're struggling (Romans 8:26).
- He will talk to God for you when you don't know what to say (Romans 8:26–27).
- He will help you say no to things that are wrong (Galatians 5:16–18).
- He will give you joy and hope (1 Thessalonians 1:6; Romans 15:13).
- And more!

Holy Father, thank You for being the perfect Dad who is always ready to listen. Thank You for sending Jesus to make a way for me to talk to You and always be with You. And thank You for your Holy Spirit, who is always with me and helps me pray when I don't know what to say. Through Jesus I pray, amen.

WHAT DO YOU THINK?

1. What is one thing that is possible only because of Jesus?

   _____

   _____

   _____

   _____

   _____

   _____

THE WHO OF PRAYER

2. Look back at the list of things the Holy Spirit does for you. What do you most need today from the Holy Spirit? Talk to God about that.

   _____

   _____

   _____

   _____

   _____

3. Think about all that God the Father, God the Son, and God the Holy Spirit do for you. What does that tell you about how big God's love for you is?

   _____

   _____

   _____

   _____

   _____

PART 2

PRAYERS TO HELP YOU PRAY

WE'RE TALKING ABOUT TALKING TO GOD

The Bible talks a lot about talking *to* God. But there aren't that many actual prayers in the Bible—except for the ones in Psalms. The prayers that *are* in the Bible, though, are great guides to help you learn to pray.

"Guide prayers" are like an outline or a blueprint for planning out your own prayers. They will help you remember everything you want to include in your prayers, like

GOD WILL GIVE YOU EVERYTHING YOU NEED TO FOLLOW HIM. YOU JUST HAVE TO ASK.

- praising God,
- telling Him about your sins and mistakes,
- asking for what you need and want, and
- praying for others.

God's Word tells us to pray all the time and in all kinds of ways (Ephesians 6:18). So let's dive into some guide prayers and explore a few of those ways.

CHAPTER 6

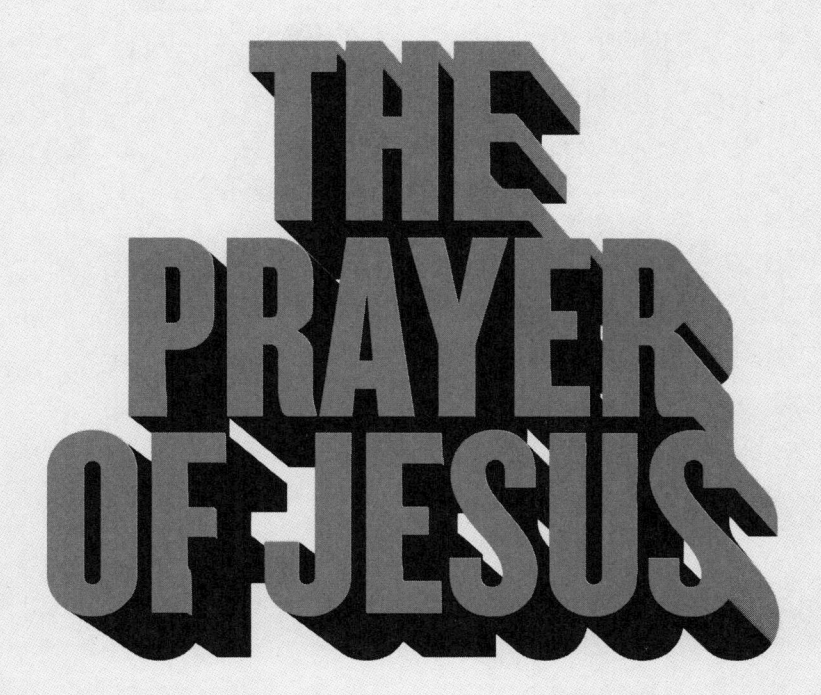

THE PRAYER OF JESUS

IT'S THE SIZE OF GOD'S LOVE THAT MATTERS, NOT THE SIZE OF YOUR WORDS.

THE BEST GUIDE

Many people memorize the Lord's Prayer—and that's great! But don't just repeat it back to God. Instead, use it as a guide to help you pray.

A Shocking Prayer

When the disciples first heard Jesus praying, they were shocked! They'd never heard anyone speak to God so personally before. It blew their minds!

Sure, the disciples grew up praying. But the Jews of that time mostly said

THE LORD'S PRAYER

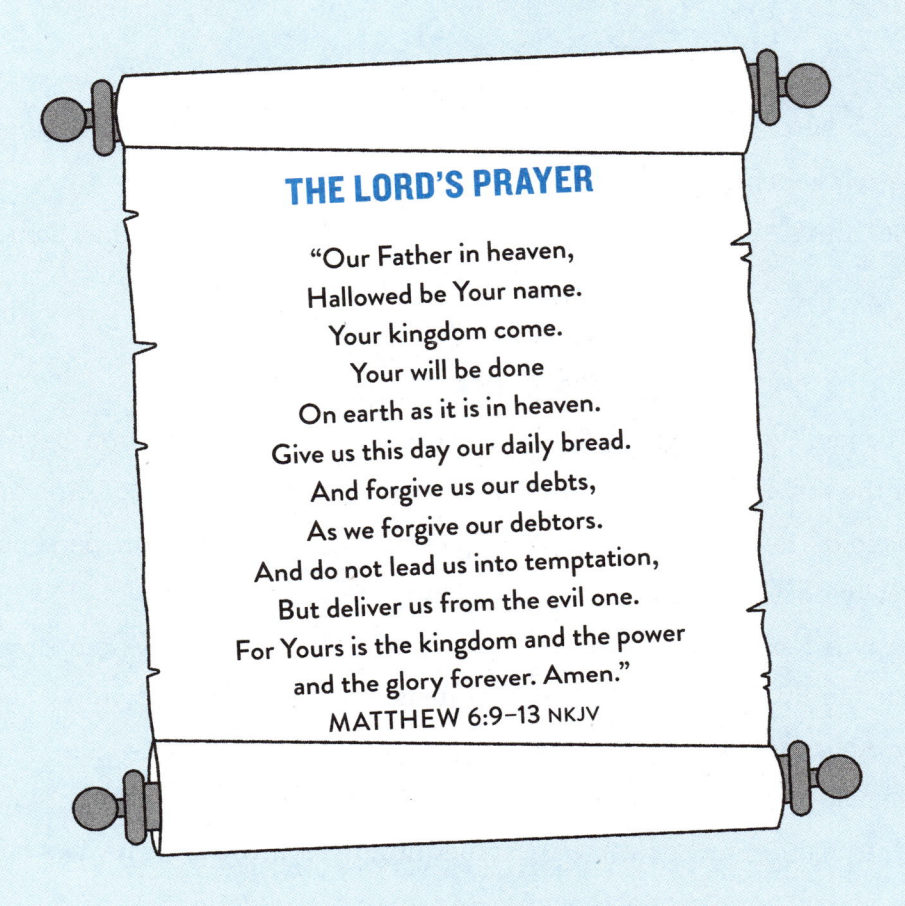

"Our Father in heaven,
Hallowed be Your name.
Your kingdom come.
Your will be done
On earth as it is in heaven.
Give us this day our daily bread.
And forgive us our debts,
As we forgive our debtors.
And do not lead us into temptation,
But deliver us from the evil one.
For Yours is the kingdom and the power
and the glory forever. Amen."
MATTHEW 6:9–13 NKJV

"official" prayers that they memorized and repeated word for word at certain times and in certain ceremonies. Jesus didn't repeat words He'd memorized, though. He actually *talked to God!*

Teach Us!

After the disciples got over the shock of Jesus' prayers, they asked Jesus to teach them to pray the way He did. That's when Jesus gave them the Lord's Prayer as an example. He not only taught them how to talk to God, but He also gave them a way to connect to God.

THE PRAYER OF JESUS

That's what God really wants from your prayers: connection. He wants to build a relationship with you.

The Lord's Prayer has seven different parts. Each part teaches something about God and talking to Him. Let's get started.

#1: START WITH HIS NAME: "OUR FATHER IN HEAVEN"

Jesus began His prayer by calling His Father's name. When you begin your prayer the same way, you're reminded of who you're talking to: God. You are also reminded of the kind of relationship God wants with you: a warm, personal, and God-really-does-want-to-hear-from-you kind of relationship.

Because here's the thing: When you choose to follow Jesus, God adopts you into His family. You become His son or daughter, and He invites you to call Him Father, Abba, or Dad (Romans 8:15).

Because God is the perfect Father, you can go to Him anytime. Not just when you're struggling or when you want something. In fact, God loves it when you stop to chat about your day or about what He's up to in the world.

Dear God, my Father, Holy Lord, my Abba . . .

WHO'S THE BOSS?

Imagine that your mom asks you to clean your room and to tell your brother to clean his room too. If you say to your brother, "Hey! Clean your room," he'll probably laugh, right? He might say, "You're not the boss of me!" But if you say, "*Mom* told me to tell you to clean your room"—well, that's a completely different story, right? Because you used the name of the person in charge, the one with the authority (Mom). That's kind of like what happens when you pray in God's name.

PRAY FIRST

HALLOWED (HAL-OHD): holy, sacred, blessed, honored

#2: WORSHIP HIS NAME: "HALLOWED BE YOUR NAME."

Hallowed probably isn't a word you and your friends use a lot. It's a great word for describing God, though, because it means *holy*, *sacred*, *blessed*, and *honored*. So when you pray "hallowed be Your name," you're saying that God's name is holy, sacred, blessed, and honored. In other words, you *worship* His name.

What's in a Name?

God's name is more than letters on a page. It has power in a way that our names don't. When you worship His name, you're asking God to pour His power into your life.

There is also safety in His name. "God's name is a place of protection—good people can run there and be safe" (Proverbs 18:10 THE MESSAGE). Just saying His name reminds you that He is with you, and it tells the Enemy to back off because you belong to God.

God's name has authority. When you pray His name, it's like declaring He is in control—that He's the boss of this situation. Which, of course, He is!

Abba Father, I'm starting this prayer with Your name! Because You are in control,

WHAT DOES THE BIBLE SAY?

Look up Luke 12:31 in the Bible. When you focus on God and on His kingdom, what does He give you?

You have all the power and authority. Lead me where You want me to go. In Jesus' name, amen.

#3: PRAYING WHAT GOD WANTS: "YOUR KINGDOM COME. YOUR WILL BE DONE ON EARTH AS IT IS IN HEAVEN."

With these words, Jesus taught His disciples to pray for the things *God* wants. This isn't the time to be all "gimme, gimme, gimme" and make it all about you. You'll have time to ask God for the things you need and want later. But for now, focus on God and what He wants.

What does God want? More than anything, He wants people to know Him and become part of His family. He wants it so much that He sent Jesus to make it possible (John 3:16). And He wants your heart to desire that too.

DON'T FORGET!

Memorize the Lord's Prayer so you can use it to guide your prayers more easily. Try memorizing just one line at a time and adding a new line each day. By doing that, you could have it all memorized in just seven days! Of course, it's okay if it takes a little longer. (God's not grading you on this.)

Dear God, so many people don't know You—even people I care about. Please change their hearts so they want to know You. And help me to have the courage to tell them about You. In Jesus' name, amen.

> ## IT'S NOT ME, IT'S YOU
>
> Want to make sure you're praying for what God wants instead of just stuff for yourself? Try this: See how many times you can use "You" (as in God) in your prayers instead of "me" and "my."

#4: REMEMBER, GOD'S GOT YOU: "GIVE US THIS DAY OUR DAILY BREAD."

Now is the time to ask God for the things you need—and even want. (And, yes, it really is okay to ask.)

When you ask God for the things you need and want, it means you understand that every good thing ultimately comes from God (James 1:17). For example, that food on your table may have come from the grocery store, but it didn't start there. It started with plants created by God, watered by rain He sent, fed by His dirt, and warmed by a sun He put in the sky.

Then, when you pray "daily," you're trusting Him to give you what you need for today—and believing He'll give you what you need for tomorrow.

HUMBLE (HUM-BUL): giving honor to God instead of trying to get it for yourself

If God Knows Everything . . .

Now, maybe you're wondering, *If God knows everything, then doesn't He already know what I need? Why do I have to ask Him?*

Great question! It's because God wants *you* to know you need Him. It shows that you trust Him. It also helps you to stay humble and grateful for all that He gives you. Remember, God will give you the things you truly need.

> *Abba Father, thank You for taking such good care of me. Every good thing I have comes from You, and I'm so grateful. And one of the very best things You've given me is a way to talk to You. In Jesus' name, amen.*

#5: GET YOUR HEART RIGHT: "FORGIVE US OUR DEBTS, AS WE FORGIVE OUR DEBTORS."

There are two parts to this "forgiving thing," and both are super important.

First Up, 'Fess Up!

Confess to, or tell, God about the wrong things you've done. Admit your sins and mistakes—and *be specific*. Yes, God already knows. But admitting that you've messed up helps you remember how *huge* God's grace is, and it helps you to be grateful for the *huge* price Jesus paid on the cross to purchase that grace for you.

You don't have to be afraid of confessing your sins to God, because He *will* forgive you. No ifs, buts, or maybes about it. Nothing you tell Him will change how much He loves you.

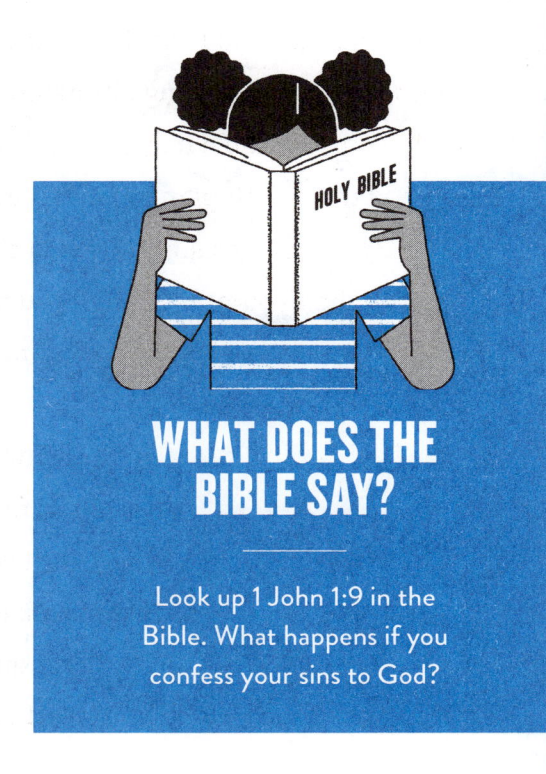

WHAT DOES THE BIBLE SAY?

Look up 1 John 1:9 in the Bible. What happens if you confess your sins to God?

Next Step, Pass It On!

Don't keep all that grace for yourself. Pass it on and forgive others for the wrong things they've said or done.

Don't miss how important this is: *If you don't forgive someone for the wrong thing they did or said, God won't forgive you* (Matthew 6:15). So don't hold a grudge. Let it go so you can receive God's grace too.

Okay, but let's be practical for a minute. Some things are much harder to forgive than others, aren't they? If your sister calls you a name, that's a lot different than being lied to or lied about—or worse. Forgiving something like that can take some time. Talk to God about it and ask for His help to forgive. That's a prayer He's always happy to answer. God will give you the strength to do what He asks you to do (Philippians 4:13).

DID YOU KNOW...?

The Lord's Prayer is so awesome that it's in the Bible *twice*—once in Matthew 6:9–13 and then in Luke 11:2–4. Sometimes it's called the "Our Father" prayer because it begins with the words "Our Father."

> Dear God, I know I messed up. I did _____, and I said _____. That was wrong. Please forgive me. And thank You for already forgiving me. Now, God, I need Your help to forgive _____. They _____, and it made me feel _____. Lord, You've forgiven me so many times. Please help me to forgive them too. In Jesus' name, amen.

#6: GOD FIGHTS FOR YOU: "AND DO NOT LEAD US INTO TEMPTATION, BUT DELIVER US FROM THE EVIL ONE."

This is where the words get a little tricky. Remember, this part of the Bible was first written in Greek, not English. So the words don't always translate quite the same. A better translation would be, "Do not allow us to be led into temptation."

You see, God doesn't *lead* you into temptation. The Enemy sure tries to, though! The Enemy will use all kinds of tricks and traps to see if he can make you trip and fall.

That's why you need to ask for God's help.

God can give you the wisdom to spot the Enemy's tricks and traps. And He can give you the strength to say no to them. Just ask Him. *Every day.* Because the devil is out setting his traps every day.

> God, please give me the wisdom to see through the Enemy's tricks and help me to spot his traps. Give me the strength to say no to those wrong things, which the Enemy makes look so good. In Jesus' name, amen.

#7: BELIEVE AND BOOST YOUR FAITH: "FOR YOURS IS THE KINGDOM AND THE POWER AND THE GLORY FOREVER."

This last part of the prayer is about telling God that you believe He is Lord and He has the power to do everything you've asked Him to do—and more! You're not telling God because He's forgotten or because He's having a tough day and needs you to cheer Him up. You're reminding yourself of how amazing, wonderful, perfect, and powerful He is.

Which is the perfect way to end your time with God.

PRAY FIRST

Lord, everything is Yours. You created it all and control it all. Nothing and no one is as powerful as You. I'm so grateful that You listen to me and help me. Thank You, God. In Jesus' name, amen.

REMEMBER . . .

Prayer is all about growing closer to God. You don't have to be all fancy or use big words. You can talk to Him like He's your Dad who knows you inside and out and who loves you without end. Could there be a better reason to . . . pray first?

WHAT DO YOU THINK?

1. Think about all the different ways people say your name when they're happy or sad or angry. How do you like to hear your name said? How does God like to hear His name said?

   _____

   _____

   _____

   _____

   _____

THE PRAYER OF JESUS

2. God wants you to forgive others just as He forgives you. Why is that so important to God? Why doesn't He want you to get even or hold a grudge?

_____

_____

_____

_____

_____

3. Which part of the Lord's Prayer is the easiest for you to pray? Which is the hardest?

_____

_____

_____

_____

_____

CHAPTER 7

THE PRAYER OF MOSES

PRAYER IS A TIME TO REMEMBER WHO GOD IS AND ALL THE REASONS YOU HAVE TO PRAISE HIM.

MOSES AND THE TABERNACLE

Do you remember Moses? He's the guy whose mom floated him down the Nile River and a princess found him and raised him as a prince of Egypt. But that's not all! There was a burning bush, a massive mission from God to rescue the Israelites, a walk through the Red Sea, and two tablets with the Ten Commandments. *Whew!* (Check out the book of Exodus to read all about Moses' amazing adventures with God.)

Well, after all that, Moses led the Israelites into the land God promised to

DID YOU KNOW...?

God gave Moses very exact instructions about how to build the tabernacle and how to enter it after it was built. Once Moses was inside, "the LORD would speak to Moses face to face, as one speaks to a friend" (Exodus 33:11 NLT). *Face to face! With God!* How amazing is that?

Even more amazing is that God invites you to do the same thing. Because of Jesus, you can meet with God personally. You might not see His face, but He'll be right there with you, just as He was with Moses.

give them. It took a *looong* time to get there—but that's a whole other story. God loved His people and wanted to be with them for every step of their trip. So He told Moses to build a tabernacle. It was like a huge tent with a smaller tent inside. Because it was a tent, they could fold it up and take it with them as they traveled. Also, the tabernacle had seven "stops"—places where Moses paused to get ready to talk to God.

You don't need the tabernacle to talk with God today. And you don't need those seven stops. However, "walking" through them can be a great way to guide your prayers and move you closer to God.

Ready? Let's start stopping!

STOP #1: THE OUTER COURT: PRAISING GOD

The first stop of your tabernacle tour is the outer court (or courtyard). This was the open area just outside the tent of the tabernacle. It's the first place Moses stopped. This place reminded Moses to praise God and thank Him for all His good gifts.

THE PRAYER OF MOSES

Gratitude is a fabulous way to start your prayers. Starting a prayer by telling God what you want and need is easy. But stopping and giving thanks first for all He's already given you helps you see how blessed you already are. Even on days that feel pretty rotten. Gratitude keeps your heart and mind headed in the right direction—closer to God.

GRATITUDE (GRAH-TIH-TUDE): being thankful for what you have

God, You are so good to me. Thank You for all the wonderful people and blessings You've poured into my life. I especially thank You for [insert what you're thankful for]. Most of all, thank You for loving me and saving me. I love You, Lord. In Jesus' name, amen.

WHAT DOES THE BIBLE SAY?

Look up Exodus 25:8–9. Why did God want the Israelites to build the tabernacle?

STOP AND PRAISE

When you're having a tough day, stop and take a deep breath. Look around and think of ten blessings you're grateful for. Count them out on your fingers. And then thank God for each one.

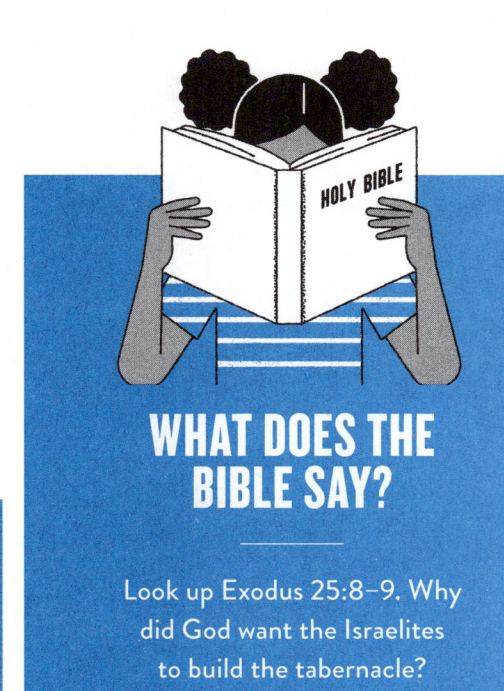

A MONTH OF PRAISE—OR MORE!

Every day for a month, think of one new blessing to praise and thank God for—no repeats. Write it in a journal or on a poster to hang on your door or wall. Can you do it for two months? Six months? A whole year?

STOP #2: THE BRONZE ALTAR: HEALING FROM SIN AND MISTAKES

Before Jesus came, God's law said that sin had to be paid for with blood. The bronze altar—the second stop—was where this happened. There, the priest sacrificed an animal—often a cow or sheep. It was an offering to God to pay for the people's sins. But this "payment" was only temporary. So the people had to keep offering more animals. But when Jesus came and died on the cross, His perfect blood paid for everyone's sins forever.

Now, instead of animals, you can offer God a sacrifice of praise. That means you take this time to thank Him for sending Jesus and making a way for you to live with Him forever.

DID YOU KNOW...?

The bronze altar (BRONZ AHL-tur) was built from acacia wood and covered with bronze. It sat in the outer court and was where the offerings of animal sacrifices were burned. These sacrifices "paid" for the people's sins.

THE PRAYER OF MOSES

God, I make so many mistakes, and I'm so sorry. Thank You, God, for sending Jesus to save me. I am so grateful You've made a way for me to be forgiven. And I'm so sorry it hurt You and Jesus so much. Please help me to be more and more like Jesus. In Jesus' name, amen.

STOP #3: THE LAVER: CLEANING UP YOUR HEART

The laver (LAY-vur) was a huge bronze bowl filled with water. Moses stopped here to wash his hands and feet before getting any closer to the holiness of God. As he dipped his hands into the water, he could see his reflection in the shiny bronze and rinse all the dirt off.

DID YOU KNOW . . . ?

The bronze laver was made of mirrors![1] But not the kind we have today. These mirrors were made of bronze that was polished until you could see your face in it. When the tabernacle was being built, women gave their mirrors to be melted down and made into the bronze laver.

The laver reminds you to ask God to clean up every part of your life. It's that one sinful part you're not sure you want to give up—like the grudge you're holding, that show you're not supposed to be watching, or your plans to cheat on that test. Tell God all your sins, and then ask Him to forgive you and make you clean.

God, I know I've sinned and messed up. Please show me the parts of my life You want me to change. I want to live my whole life for You, and I can't wait to see what You have planned for me. In Jesus' name, amen.

SPIRITUAL GIFTS

What are *spiritual gifts*? They are gifts—or talents—given to you by the Holy Spirit. These talents are different from ones like painting or playing sports or juggling bowling balls. (Though you absolutely can use those talents to share God with others!) Spiritual gifts are things like these:

- Serving
- Teaching
- Encouraging
- Giving
- Leading
- Being kind

Read more about spiritual gifts in Romans 12:4–8.

STOP #4: THE CANDLESTICK: FILLING YOUR LIFE WITH LIGHT

The fourth stop in Moses' walk took him inside the tabernacle to a candlestick. This was no ordinary candlestick. It had seven branches for seven burning lights and was called a menorah (meh-NOR-uh).

Think about the fire in those burning lights for a moment. Fire gives light, warmth, and comfort. So does the Spirit of God. Perhaps that's why fire so often represents the Spirit of God in the Bible, like the burning bush that Moses saw, the pillar of fire that led the Israelites through the wilderness, and the tongues of fire in Acts 2:2–4.

The candlestick reminds you to invite the Holy Spirit of God to work in your life. (Read more about what the Holy Spirit does in chapter 5.) Here you can ask God to use your life for His purposes, show you the spiritual gifts He's given you, and help you use those gifts to help others and serve Him. You can even ask Him to give you spiritual gifts so you can serve Him more!

THE PRAYER OF MOSES

Father God, please fill me with Your Holy Spirit. Help me to see all the ways that You are working in my life. Teach me to recognize and use the gifts You've given. And help me to love others the way You love them. In Jesus' name, amen.

STOP #5: THE TABLE OF SHOWBREAD: FILLING UP AND FUELING UP ON GOD'S PROMISES

Moses' next stop was at a nearby table that had twelve loaves of freshly baked bread stacked on it. (It must have smelled amazing!) This bread reminds you to fill yourself up with the promises found in God's Word.

Jesus said, "People do not live by bread alone, but by every word that comes from the mouth of God" (Matthew 4:4 NLT). And Jesus said that *after* He had fasted and not eaten any food for forty days in the desert! So you know God's Word must be extra good and satisfying!

Just as our bodies need food to keep us strong, our spirits also need God's Word. When you feast on His Word every day (also known as reading it), it keeps you healthy and strong. And it helps you become more and more like Jesus. (Find a few of God's promises in chapter 4).

Before you begin to read God's Word, pray: Thank You, God, for the gift of the Bible. As I read through Your words today,

WHAT DOES THE BIBLE SAY?

Look up Isaiah 53:5 in the Bible. How are you healed from your sins?

79

AS YOU PRAY . . .

- Touch your head and ask God to fill your mind with thoughts of Him and all the good things you can do with and for Him.
- Touch your eyes and ask God to help you focus on Him and on seeing those you can help.
- Touch your ears and ask God to fill your ears with His truth and shut out the Enemy's lies.
- Touch your mouth and ask God to help you say only helpful and encouraging words.
- Touch your hands and ask God to help you do good things for others.
- Touch your feet and ask God to lead you where He wants you to go.

please show me what You want me to learn. Teach me more about who You are, how to love You, and how to help the people You love. In Jesus' name, amen.

STOP #6: THE ALTAR OF INCENSE: TAKING TIME TO WORSHIP

Next, Moses went to the altar of incense. It stood just outside the holy of holies (the smaller tent inside the big one), where God's presence lived. A sweet-smelling incense burned on this altar night and day as a way to worship God.

> **INCENSE (IN-SENTS):** spices and oils that produce a fragrance when burned

Today your worship is the incense. Your praises smell sweet to God. In the outer court part of this prayer (stop #1), you thanked God for all He has done. Now, you're thanking God for who He

THE PRAYER OF MOSES

is. Praise Him as your Father, your Creator, the One who loves you, and the One who saves you. In other words, praise God for being God.

> Lord, You are good and holy and perfect in all that You do. You are my Counselor and Friend. You heal my hurts, defend me, protect me, and make sure I have everything I need. You never, ever leave me. For all that and for so much more, I praise You and thank You. I love You, God. In Jesus' name, amen.

STOP # 7: THE MERCY SEAT: PRAYING FOR OTHERS

The last stop for Moses was inside the holy of holies. This was the holiest place in the tabernacle. It's where the ark of the covenant sat. This ark was a box made of wood and covered in gold. Two golden angels were on top, and between them was the mercy seat. The presence of God came down and "sat" on the mercy seat to meet with Moses.

When you come to this part of the prayer, it's time to pray for others. Talk to Him about those who are sick or hurting or who need His help in some way. Pray for your leaders—at home, at school, at church, and in the government. Ask God to heal the broken places and broken people in the world.

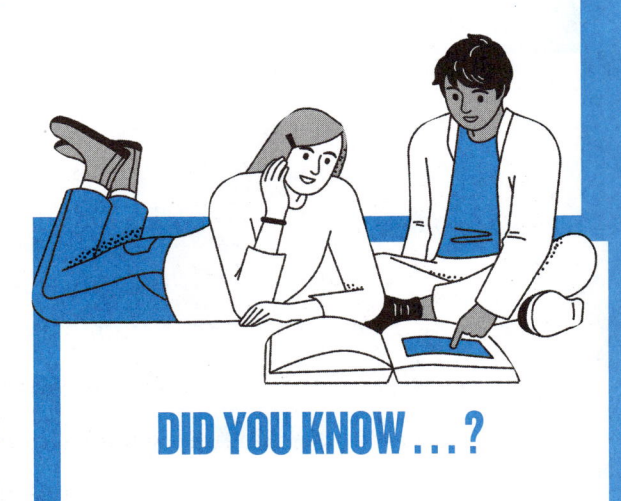

DID YOU KNOW...?

The word *worship* comes from the same root word as *worth*. When you worship the Lord, you are praising Him for His worth—which is greater than you could ever imagine!

Thank You, God, for the people You've put in my life. Watch over them, protect them, and bless them. I especially pray for [name those who have a specific need]. I know that You will take good care of them and that You will also take good care of me. Thank You, God. In Jesus' name, amen.

WHO AND WHAT ARE IN YOUR PRAYERS?

Do you ever stop to pray and suddenly can't remember what you should pray? To help you remember, take some index cards and write these six categories, one on each card. Under that, write the specific people and things you want to talk to God about.

- **PRAISE AND THANKS:** Praise God for how wonderful He is, and thank Him for His blessings. (Be specific!)
- **FAMILY AND FRIENDS:** Write down any specific needs or thoughts you have about those closest to you.
- **CHURCH:** Church leaders, teachers, and members need your prayers. Add any special events that might be coming up.
- **LEADERS:** From your school to your community to the whole world, pray that leaders would turn to God and learn from His wisdom.
- **OTHER PEOPLE:** Are there other people in your community who need your prayers?
- **YOURSELF:** Don't forget to pray for yourself! Ask God for the things you need and want. Ask Him to help you be a blessing to others. You can even ask God to make your faith stronger.

THE PRAYER OF MOSES

REMEMBER . . .

Moses took all these steps so he could talk to God. However, because of Jesus, you don't *have* to take any of them. God is always ready to listen to you, especially when you . . . pray first!

WHAT DO YOU THINK?

1. What was the most interesting thing you learned about the tabernacle?

   _____

   _____

   _____

   _____

   _____

   _____

   _____

PRAY FIRST

2. How does it feel to know that you can talk to God anytime—without going through any of the seven steps Moses had to take?

_____

_____

_____

_____

_____

3. What do you want to praise God for most today?

_____

_____

_____

_____

_____

_____

CHAPTER 8

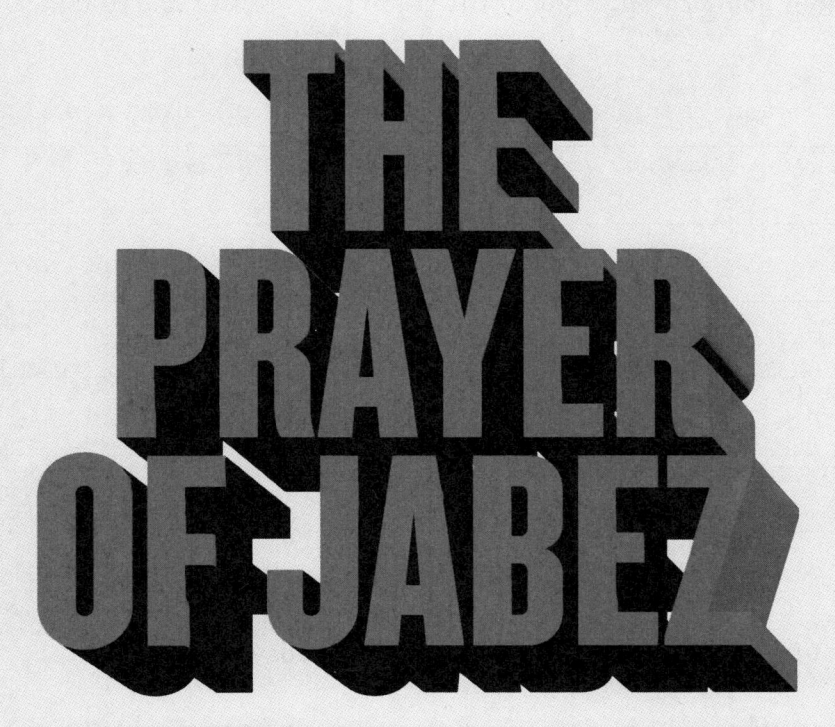

THE PRAYER OF JABEZ

GOD BLESSES YOU SO YOU CAN BLESS OTHERS.

LITTLE WORDS WITH A POWERFUL PUNCH

The prayer of Jabez isn't long, but it packs a powerful punch. You can pray through it quickly in just a couple of minutes. Or you can spend a little more time on each of its four parts.

WHO EXACTLY WAS JABEZ?

Jabez only pops up once in the entire Bible. In 1 Chronicles 4:9–10, to be exact. You'll find his name right smack in the middle of all these impossible-to-pronounce names, such as Hazzobebah and Shuhah. Here's how this little passage about Jabez starts:

> Jabez was more honorable than his brothers. His mother had named him Jabez, saying, "I gave birth to him in pain." (1 Chronicles 4:9 NIV)

That's right. Jabez's mom named him the Hebrew word that sounds like "pain." *Yikes! Thanks, Mom!*

Have you ever been labeled with a name or nickname? Like "quiet kid" or "sports guy" or "science nerd"? Some labels can be tough to live with, like "pain."

Something is cool about Jabez's name, though. In ancient times, your name could define you *for life*. (Hang on—that's *not* the cool part.) But after you read Jabez's prayer, you'll see that he wasn't willing to settle for a life of pain. He asked God for something so much bigger and better than what the world expected from him—and so can you. Whether or not your name means pain.

And guess what? "God granted his request" (1 Chronicles 4:10 NIV).

BIBLE NAMES

Check out the meanings of these names found in the Bible.[1]

- **ABIGAIL:** my father's joy
- **DANIEL:** God is my judge
- **ESAU:** hairy
- **GABRIEL:** God is my strength
- **HAGAR:** flight
- **HANNAH:** grace
- **NABAL:** fool
- **SARAH:** princess

A FOUR-PART PRAYER

In just a few words—only one verse in the Bible—Jabez prayed for four things:

- Blessing
- Influence
- God's presence
- Protection

Let's take a look at what exactly he asked for—and why God was willing to say "Yes!" to all four.

#1: PRAYER FOR BLESSING: "OH, THAT YOU WOULD BLESS ME."

"Bless me" comes from the Hebrew word *barak* (baw-RAK). It means "to kneel or stoop down."[2] Jabez began by asking God to stoop down from heaven and touch his life. To bless him.

> **DON'T FORGET!**
>
> Jabez cried out to the God of Israel, "Oh, that you would bless me and enlarge my territory! Let your hand be with me, and keep me from harm so that I will be free from pain." And God granted his request.
> —1 Chronicles 4:10 NIV

What Blessing Is Not

Some people think if they just ask God to bless them, then He will. They believe that if they name something they want, then they can claim that God will bring that blessing into their lives. But this "name it and claim it" concept treats God like a vending machine—drop in your prayer (coin), and out pops your blessing (a candy bar).

God doesn't work that way.

What Blessing Is

God wants to bless you with good things. In fact, He wants to flood your life with His goodness. Not so that you can be rich, have an indoor pool, and have someone to do all your chores for you. No, God wants to bless you so "you will be a blessing to others" (Genesis 12:2). He wants you to take all the goodness He's poured into your life and use it to help someone else.

Most of the time people ask for blessings so they can be happier or richer or better off *themselves*. Be different. Ask God to bless you so you can be a blessing to others.

DID YOU KNOW...?

There's something else that God stoops or bends down to do. God Himself "bends down to listen" to you when you pray (Psalm 116:2 NLT).

BE A BLESSING

Take a look around you at all the blessings you have—whether that's clothes or sports equipment, time, talents, or even money. Think of at least one way you can use your blessings to bless someone else this week.

Then do it again next week. And the next week. And the next week. And... well, you get the picture.

> Lord, please bless me. Bless me with even more than I need so I can share the blessings with others. And then teach me how to use all Your good gifts to bless others. In Jesus' name, amen.

#2: PRAYER FOR INFLUENCE: "ENLARGE MY TERRITORY."

Yes, Jabez asked for more land—but not for the reason you might think. It wasn't about having more land. It was about having more *influence*.

In Jabez's time, the owner of the land decided how the people living on his land were treated. Some landowners were harsh and treated people badly. But Jabez knew that the more land he owned, the more people he could show the goodness of God to. He could make their lives better. He could make a difference.

You don't need land to have influence. Think about your relationships—the circle of people you know and people who listen to you. Ask God to expand your territory—to make your circle of influence bigger and bigger. Not so you can be popular but so you can show His love and kindness to more and more people. So you can make a difference in their lives.

> God, please "expand my territory." Help me to be a better friend, a better classmate, a better teammate, and a better leader so others will listen when I tell them about You. Teach me how to make a difference in the lives of the people around me. In Jesus' name, amen.

INFLUENCE (IN-FLU-ENTS): the power to change a person or a situation

> ## DREAMING WITH GOD
>
> Did you know that you can dream while you pray? You can let your imagination wander. Here's how it works: Ask for a blessing. Then ask God to show you what He wants you to do with that blessing.
>
> It might not happen right away. Keep asking. Keep trusting. And be ready to follow where God leads you.

#3: PRAYER FOR GOD'S PRESENCE: "LET YOUR HAND BE WITH ME."

When the Bible says, "The hand of the Lord," it isn't talking about an actual *hand* like the ones you have. It means God's presence and power. So when Jabez prayed, "Let your hand be with me," he was asking for God's presence and power to be with him.

When you ask God to bless you and expand your circle of influence, you'll quickly realize it's all too big for you to handle on your own. You need His help to show you what to do with all those blessings and to help you make good choices with your influence.

But don't worry! This is a prayer He loves to answer! God *wants* to be with you and help you do amazing—even impossible—things.

> Lord, I believe You have a plan for me and a purpose for all these blessings You've given me. But I can't do this on my own. Please be with me every second and guide every step I take. In Jesus' name, amen.

#4: PRAYER FOR PROTECTION: "KEEP ME FROM HARM."

When God gives you blessings and influence, and when He fills your life with His presence, that's so great! But there's also some bad news: The Enemy is not going to like that one bit. In fact, he's going to attack. That's why you need to pray like Jabez and ask God to keep you from harm.

You might even be under attack right this second. (Because the Enemy isn't going to like you reading a book about prayer, is he?) For example, are you having trouble focusing on the page? Do you keep getting distracted? Does your mind keep wandering to other things? It could be a spiritual attack.

The last thing the devil wants is for you to experience everything God has planned for you—His blessings, His influence, and His presence in your life. So whatever you're praying for, it's always a good idea to ask for God's protection too.

> Lord, the more I do what You want me to do, the more the Enemy is going to attack. Please help me to be strong. Keep me safe and protect me. Don't let me or those I love be hurt or put in danger. Don't let me be tempted to do wrong. Thank You for watching over me. I love You, and I trust You to keep me safe. In Jesus' name, amen.

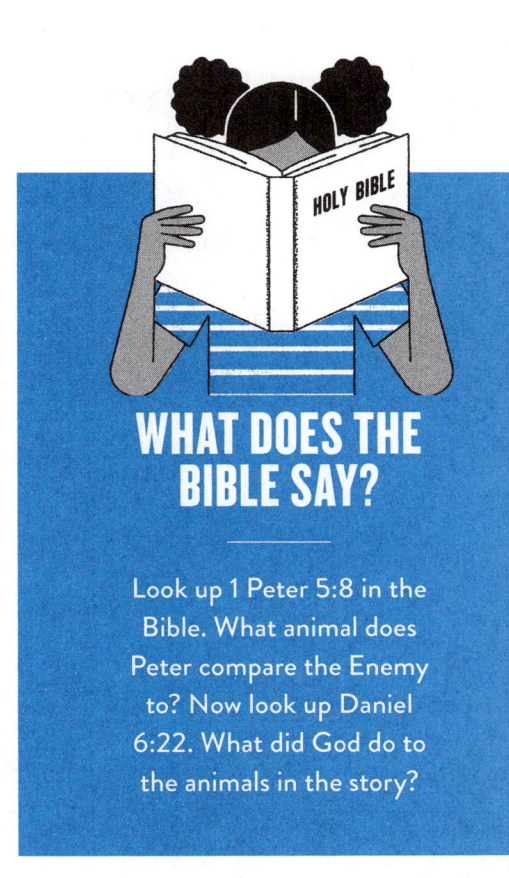

WHAT DOES THE BIBLE SAY?

Look up 1 Peter 5:8 in the Bible. What animal does Peter compare the Enemy to? Now look up Daniel 6:22. What did God do to the animals in the story?

PRAY FIRST

REMEMBER . . .

Rather than settle for the life and the label of pain his name gave him, Jabez prayed—not just for himself but for ways to help others. And God answered his prayer! Jabez's prayer shows what a difference it can make when you focus on what God wants . . . and pray first!

WHAT DO YOU THINK?

1. How can you use your blessings to bless someone today?

   _____

   _____

   _____

   _____

   _____

   _____

   _____

2. Think about your circle of influence. How can you help those people get closer to God?

_____

_____

_____

_____

_____

3. Jabez knew he didn't want his life to be about pain. (Who does?) So he asked God to change his life. What do you want your life to be about?

_____

_____

_____

_____

_____

CHAPTER 9

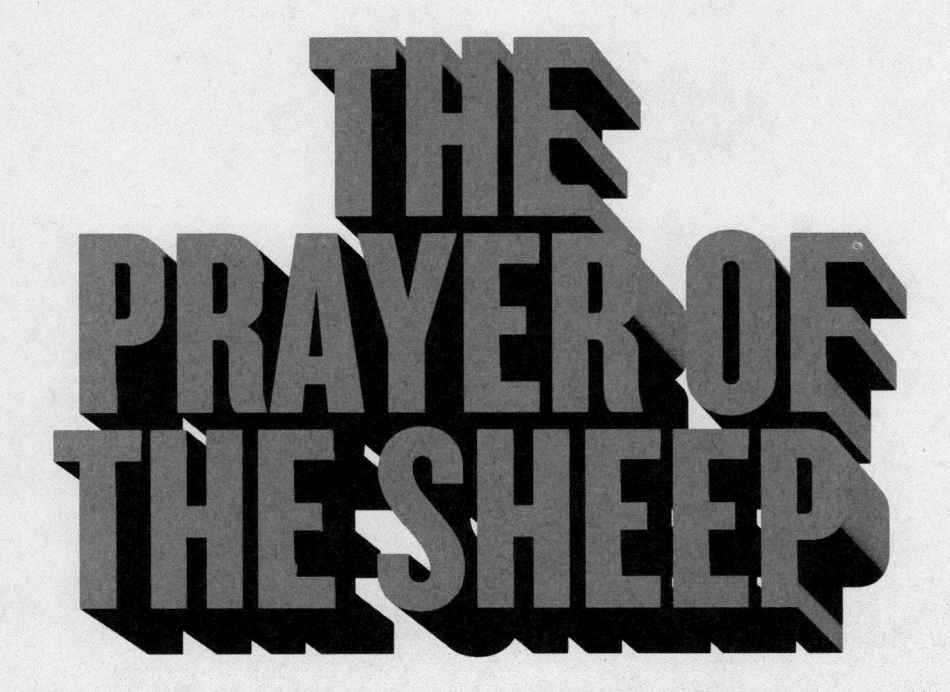

THE PRAYER OF THE SHEEP

PRAYING GOD'S NAMES HELPS YOU REMEMBER WHO HE IS AND ALL THAT HE CAN DO.

IT'S ALL IN THE NAME

You have a few different names, right? There's your first name—the name your parents gave you. There's your last name, which tells a little more about who you are. And in the middle, there's your, well, there's your middle name. You might also have a nickname. Think about the names your grandparents call you or what your friends call you. How about classmates, teachers, or coaches? What do they call you? (Not the joking names. Let's just focus on the good stuff.) Each of those names tells a little bit more about who you are.

PSALM 23

The Lord is my shepherd.
I have everything I need.
He gives me rest in green pastures.
He leads me to calm water.
He gives me new strength.
For the good of his name,
he leads me on paths that are right.
Even if I walk
through a very dark valley,
I will not be afraid
because you are with me.
Your rod and your shepherd's staff comfort me.
You prepare a meal for me
in front of my enemies.
You pour oil of blessing on my head.
You give me more than I can hold.
Surely your goodness and love will be with me
all my life.
And I will live in the house of the Lord forever.
PSALM 23:1-6

In the same way, God has more than one name. And each name tells us a little bit more about who He is.

PRAYING THROUGH THE NAMES OF GOD

Using the different names of God to pray pleases Him and helps you learn more about Him. And it also stops you from falling into the trap of making your prayers all about you.

Think about it: Have you ever been around someone who just couldn't stop

THE PRAYER OF THE SHEEP

talking about themselves? Maybe you tried to listen and be polite. But that kind of thing gets old really fast, right?

Don't misunderstand, though. God *wants* to listen to you. He *wants* to hear everything you want to tell Him—your troubles and struggles, the things you want and need, and even just random stuff about your day. But *you* are not the *only* thing He wants to hear about.

Using His names to pray takes the focus off you and puts it on Him. It's like you're declaring, "I know this is who You are, God, and I know You have the power to do this."

Praying God's names reminds you of who God is and what He can do.

SHEEP, MEET YOUR SHEPHERD

In the Bible, you find a bunch of different names of God. But eight names pop up over and over again. All eight of those names are packed inside one psalm: Psalm 23. It's all about how Jesus is the Good Shepherd and how He takes care of His sheep (also known as God's people).

#1: YOU ARE MY SHEPHERD

Jehovah-Raah (jeh-HO-vuh RAW): "The Lord is my shepherd" (v. 1).

This name of God pops up in the very first line. Right away, you learn that as your Shepherd, God will lead you, take care

DON'T FORGET!

The Lord is my shepherd.
I have everything I need.
—Psalm 23:1

WHAT DOES THE BIBLE SAY?

Look up Philippians 4:19 in the Bible. How many of your needs will God take care of?

of you, and protect you. Your job—as His sheep—is to listen when He speaks and to follow wherever He leads you.

Lord, You are my Shepherd, and I will follow You! In Jesus' name, amen.

#2: YOU ARE MY PROVIDER

Jehovah-Jireh (jeh-HO-vuh JI-reh): "I have everything I need" (v. 1).

When You pray to God as Jehovah-Jireh, you declare that you trust Him to give you everything you need.

So many people trust in money, jobs, possessions, or other people to take care of them. They believe storing up huge piles of money and buying lots of stuff is the way to go. But money can be stolen or lost, and stuff gets broken and worn out. Only God can truly take care of you.

This name of God also encourages you to share with others. When you know God will take care of you, you don't have to hold on to possessions "just in case" you need them. You can be generous because you know God will give you everything you need.

Lord, You are Jehovah-Jireh. I know that You will make sure I have everything I need—so much that I can share with others. Thank You, Lord! In Jesus' name, amen.

#3: YOU ARE MY PEACE

Jehovah-Shalom (jeh-HO-vuh shah-lohm): "God is our peace" (v. 2).

This peaceful name of God is found in the words: "He gives me rest in green pastures. He leads me to calm water" (Psalm 23:2).

The world tells you to be busy, busy, busy. Play another sport, try another hobby, do the extra work. But praying to Jehovah-Shalom reminds you that God wants you to rest. That might mean taking a nap, spending a quiet day with friends and family, or slipping away to talk to God alone.

When you rest with God, He gives you His peace.

SHALOM (SHAH-LOME): peace, but also describes being whole, complete, and well

WHAT DOES THE BIBLE SAY?

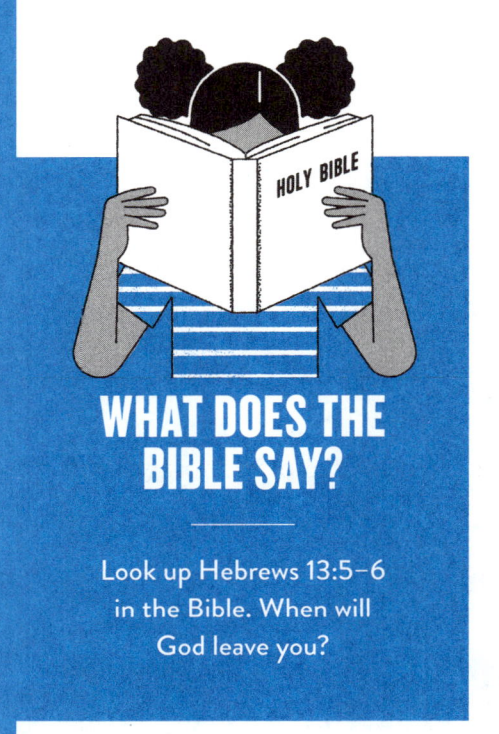

Look up Hebrews 13:5–6 in the Bible. When will God leave you?

This kind of peace is more than just not being busy. It's a sort of miraculous feeling of being safe and secure with absolutely zero need to worry or be afraid (John 14:27). Sounds pretty awesome, right?

So the next time you're feeling stressed out and maxed out, stop and have a conversation with Jehovah-Shalom.

God, You are Jehovah-Shalom. You *are* peace. Please help me stop being so busy for a little while and just rest with You. I trust You to watch over me and fill me with Your peace. In Jesus' name, amen.

#4: YOU ARE MY HEALER

Jehovah-Rapha (jeh-HO-vuh RA-fa): "God is our Healer" (v. 3).

This name of God probably makes you think of being hurt or sick and needing a doctor. But this is much more than healing your body. The Jehovah-Rapha kind of healing means God gives you new strength and restores you—He returns you back to who He created you to be. As Jehovah-Rapha, God has the power to heal your heart, mind, family, friendships—everything!

Sometimes God heals you Himself. But more often, He uses other people to encourage and help you to heal. Do you know what that means? God can also use *you* to encourage and help others heal. In other words, you could be the answer to someone's prayers.

THE PRAYER OF THE SHEEP

Lord, You know my hurts. Please heal me and make my heart whole. And please use me to help someone else feel better too. In Jesus' name, amen.

#5: YOU ARE MY RIGHTEOUSNESS

Jehovah-Tsidkenu (jeh-HO-vuh tzid-KAY-noo): "The Lord is our righteousness" (v. 3).

To be righteous means to be perfect. It means you never sin, never mess up, never make a mistake. Not possible! Perfection isn't possible for anyone. Well, except One. Jesus.

Jesus not only lived the perfect, righteous life, but He also offers to give you His righteousness and take away all your sins and mistakes. He makes you perfect in the eyes of God. When you follow God's path for your life, He'll help you become more and more like Him.

So the question is: Are you following God's path for your life? Maybe you're not quite sure what that path is. That's where prayer comes in. (You probably saw that one coming, didn't you?)

Your Shepherd will always lead you in the right direction. Why? "For the good of his name" (v. 3). Because that's who God is and what He does.

Praying to Jehovah-Tsidkenu means that you choose to follow His plans for your life instead of your own plans. (Spoiler alert: God's plans are always so much better!)

Jehovah-Tsidkenu, You are good and perfect in every way. Please cover me with Your goodness and perfection. Take away my sins. Show me Your path for my life and help me to follow it today and every day. In Jesus' name, amen.

RIGHTEOUSNESS (RI-CHUS-NES): good and right; without sin; perfect[1]

#6: YOU ARE MY CONSTANT COMPANION

Jehovah-Shammah (jeh-HO-vuh sham-MAHW): "The Lord is there" (v. 4).

When you decide to follow God, you are never alone. He is always there with you. The psalmist said it this way, "Even if I walk through a very dark valley, I will not be afraid because you are with me. Your rod and your shepherd's staff comfort me" (v. 4).

Wherever you are—in your room, in the hallways at school, on the playing field, in the library, or around your neighborhood—God is with you. Everywhere you go, He watches over you and protects you.

Abba, I know that I am never alone because You are Jehovah-Shammah. Because You are always with me, I never have to face anything alone. Thank You, God, for loving me so much. In Jesus' name, amen.

#7: YOU ARE MY DEFENDER

Jehovah-Nissi (jeh-HO-vuh nee-SEE): "God is our banner" (v. 5).

DID YOU KNOW...?

The "rod and staff" in Psalm 23:4 can be confusing. They sound like punishment, right? But God doesn't hit you with a rod if you wander off His path. No! The rod and staff are the Shepherd's tools to protect you. He uses them to fight off enemies and attackers. David, the author of this psalm, may have used a rod and staff when he fought off those lions and bears he talked about in 1 Samuel 17:34–37.

THE PRAYER OF THE SHEEP

Psalm 23:5 says, "You prepare a meal for me in front of my enemies." What does this mean? Will there be tacos? Maybe.

Basically, this verse means that you can relax even in the middle of one of life's battles. Because God is right with you and never stops fighting for you. So you can sit down and enjoy your meal as His banner of love covers you and protects you.

You can sit down, rest, be fed with God's promises (BYOT: Bring your own tacos), and get your strength back. Right in front of your enemies.

And while you're at God's table, the Enemy can't touch you.

Father God—Jehovah-Nissi—cover me with Your love and Your protection. Defend me and fight for me. I trust You to keep me safe from my enemies. In Jesus' name, amen.

#8: YOU MAKE ME HOLY

Jehovah-M'Kaddesh (jeh-HO-vuh meh-KAD-esh): "The Lord makes me holy" (v. 5).

When verse 5 talks about the "oil of blessing" being poured on your

DID YOU KNOW...?

In battle, one soldier carried an army's banner. The other soldiers all gathered around the banner. And when they were in battle, they watched it to know which way to go. It helped them remember who they were and what they fought for.

God is like our banner. We gather around Him. And when the day is tough (or even when it isn't), we can look to Him to know which way to go. He helps us remember who we are and why we are battling to be more and more like Him.

103

head, it's talking about *anointing*. God anoints those who belong to Him, who are set apart for His special, sacred use.

When you choose to follow God, He anoints you so you belong to Him and are set apart for His special, sacred use. In Old Testament times, only a few were chosen and anointed—usually, the priests. But because Jesus came, anyone who chooses to love and follow Him is anointed. Also, instead of having oil poured over your head, you have the Holy Spirit poured into you. Way less messy.

When you're anointed, God gives you a mission—a job to do for Him. He also equips you with His Holy Spirit. He makes sure you have everything you need to complete the mission—or missions—He gives you.

> Lord, anoint me—pour the oil of Your blessing on my head. Make me holy so I can serve You. Guide me to the missions You have for me. I know You will be with me, helping me and giving me everything I need. In Jesus' name, amen.

NAMES OF GOD SHIELD

Create a large shield from a piece of poster board. On it write all these names of God and what they mean. Hang it in your Prayer Spot or somewhere you will see it often. Each time you see it, remember that all these different parts of God stand like a shield between you and the Enemy.

THE PRAYER OF THE SHEEP

REMEMBER . . .

Praying the names of God helps you focus on who God is and all that He is willing and able to do in your life. It shows that you trust that His "goodness and love" will be with you all of your life (v. 6). It's one of the most powerful ways to pray and a fabulous way to . . . pray first!

WHAT DO YOU THINK?

1. What do all these names of God tell you about God and His power?

   _____

   _____

   _____

   _____

   _____

   _____

   _____

PRAY FIRST

2. Which name of God is your favorite? Why?

   _____

   _____

   _____

   _____

   _____

3. These names of God remind you of who He is and what He can do. What could make you forget that?

   _____

   _____

   _____

   _____

   _____

CHAPTER 10
THE PRAYERS FOR THE LOST

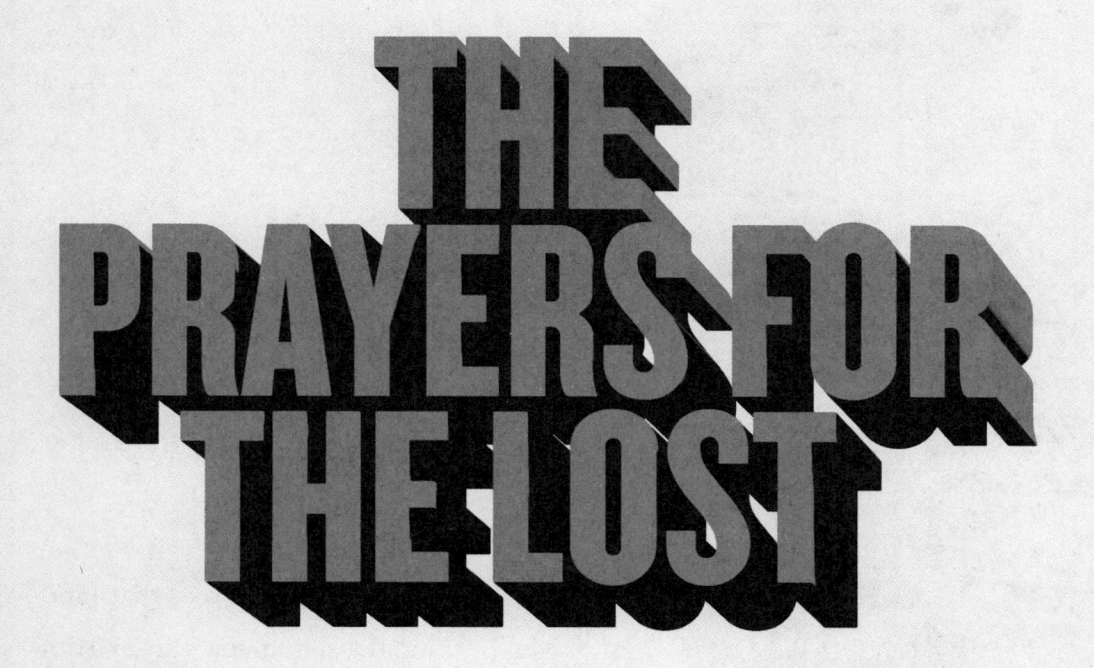

GOD SENT JESUS TO FIND THOSE WHO ARE LOST AND TO BRING THEM HOME TO HIM.

WHAT GOD WANTS MORE THAN ANYTHING

God already has the whole world, the whole universe, and everything in it. But He still wants one thing more than anything else: God wants everyone to know Him. *Everyone.* (Yes, that bully from school too!)

Is there someone in your life who doesn't know God? Someone you love and care about? Here's the thing: God loves that person even more than you do. He's chasing after them night and day with His love in so many ways. And He wants you to chase after them too. A powerful way you can do that is with your prayers.

WHAT DOES THE BIBLE SAY?

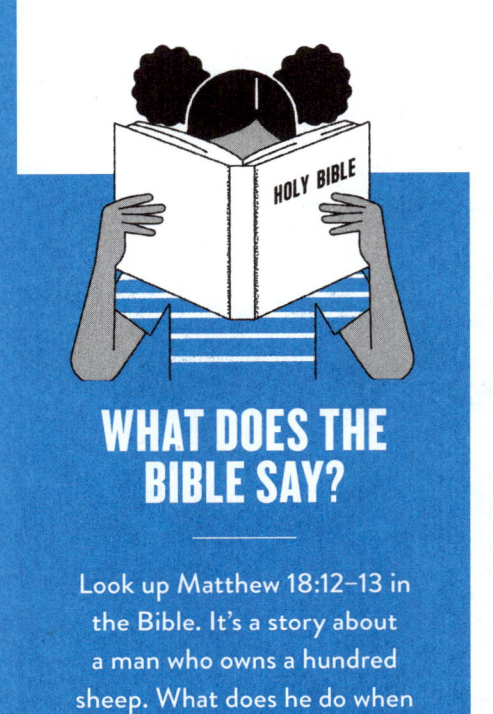

Look up Matthew 18:12–13 in the Bible. It's a story about a man who owns a hundred sheep. What does he do when one sheep wanders off? What does he do when he finds it? (*Psst!* God is like that man!)

God wants you to partner with Him to pray for those who are lost and don't know Him. (How cool is that? *Partners with God!*) Here are some ways you can do that.

#1: ASK GOD TO PULL THOSE PEOPLE CLOSER TO HIM

God loves to pull people closer to Him. He's also the only One who can do it. Jesus said, "No one can come to me unless the Father draws him to me" (John 6:44).

In other words, *you* can't make someone decide to love God. You don't have that kind of power. But God does, and you *can* ask Him to use that power to open up their hearts and pull them closer to Him.

Abba, today I'm thinking about [name]. I know You love them, and You want them to come to You. So please pull their heart closer to You. Help them see how much they need You. In Jesus' name, amen.

#2: ASK GOD TO PULL OFF THEIR BLINDFOLDS

It might sound crazy, but a lot of people are walking around wearing blindfolds. Okay, not actual blindfolds covering their eyes but spiritual blindfolds that keep them from seeing God. They go through life bumping into Him and all the ways He's working in their lives—and they can't even see that it's Him!

HOW DO YOU KNOW?

How do you know who you should pray for? How do you know whether or not someone knows God? After all, you don't want to be all judgy about it, but you also don't want to skip praying for someone who really needs it. What do you do?

Ask God. (*Psst!* That's pretty much always a good answer.) He'll put someone in your thoughts who needs your prayers. Also, look around. Notice what words people say and how they treat you. Not because you're judging them, but to look for people who might need your prayers.

Guess who put those blindfolds on them. Yep. The Enemy. He also likes to stop up their ears so they can't hear God's voice.

But you know the One who is stronger than the Enemy: God! He can snatch off blindfolds and unstop their ears. Just ask.

> God, please chase away the Enemy who is trying so hard to keep [name] from knowing You. Snatch off the blindfold so they can see You and know who You are. Open their ears to hear You, and open their heart to love You. In Jesus' name, amen.

#3: ASK GOD TO HELP THEM MEET HIM PERSONALLY

Many people think that being a Christian is just like being part of any other religion. Those phony gods of other religions don't care about the people who worship them. So people think that maybe God doesn't care either. Or that He's just anxious to punish them for every little mistake they've ever made. *They are so wrong!*

People believe these lies because they haven't personally met God yet. You can pray for that to happen.

Because when people personally meet God, they realize that God is real and He cares. He cares so much that He sent Jesus to make sure everyone has a chance to be part of His family.

You see, when you invite Jesus into your life, God adopts you into His family. He knows you perfectly, inside and out. And He loves you perfectly, inside and out.

God wants to have that kind of relationship with every single person on earth. And it starts when they meet Him personally for the first time. You can help by showing God's love to everyone around you. And you can help by praying.

God, please help _____ see that You're not some angry judge anxious to punish them for every little mistake. Put a longing in their heart to know You, to hear Your voice, and to be adopted into Your family. Help them see that as soon as they take one

DID YOU KNOW...?

These days, *salty* can mean upset or snarky. But in Bible times, it meant something completely different.[1] Back then, no one had a refrigerator. And there wasn't any ice in the desert. To keep meat from going bad, people used salt. It preserved their food, and it also added flavor.

When Jesus told believers to be salt in the world, He meant *we* should preserve and add flavor. *Preserve* their souls by introducing others to Jesus, the One who can save them from evil. And *add flavor* to the world with our kindness, patience, peace, and joy. In other words, stay salty!

THE PRAYERS FOR THE LOST

step toward You, they'll see You running to welcome them into Your family. In Jesus' name, amen.

#4: ASK GOD TO SHOW YOU HOW TO BE SALT AND LIGHT

Have you ever noticed that God will bring just the right person into your life at just the right moment? Maybe a friend comes along when you're having a tough morning. Maybe you hear the perfect Bible verse just when you need it. Or maybe it's as simple as a stranger sharing a smile on a gloomy day.

God uses His people to encourage His people. He also uses His people to reach out to those who don't know Him. That's what Jesus was talking about when He said we need to be salt and light in the world (Matthew 5:13–16).

The More You Know God

The more you know God, the more you'll want to share Him with the people around you. Sometimes that means talking about Him, sharing a Bible verse, or sharing a prayer. Other times, though, it means being kind, patient, and willing to help without getting anything in return. In other words, it means living like Jesus. People will start to notice that you're different from the world, and they'll want to know why you live that way. That's when you'll get to tell them about Jesus.

DON'T FORGET!

"Let your light shine before others, that they may see your good deeds and glorify your Father in heaven."
—Matthew 5:16 NIV

You can also ask God to send more and more of His people into the life of that person you're praying for. And ask God to help you be salt and light.

> Father, please send so many other Christians into _____'s life today so that they just have to see that You are the One doing it. Give those other believers the right words to say to help _____ see how much they need You. And help me be salt and light to everyone I meet. Let my words and actions show others how much I love You and how much You love them. In Jesus' name, amen.

#5: ASK GOD FOR WISDOM

Everyone has an empty spot inside that needs to be filled. No, not in your stomach. It's an empty spot in your heart and soul.

Some people try to fill up that empty spot with money and stuff. Others try fame or popularity or worse things like drugs. Some of those things might even seem to work for a little while. But sooner or later, people end up feeling empty again. That's because only God can fully and forever fill that empty spot.

But people need wisdom to see that God is the answer. And that kind of wisdom only comes from God. So pray that God will give them the wisdom to see how much they need Him . . . to love them, to forgive them, and to walk through their whole life with them.

WISDOM: the ability to know what is good and right and true (wisdom comes from God)[2]

> God, I pray for _____. Please give them Your wisdom. Help them see how much they need Jesus to wash away their sins. Help them understand how much You love them and that only You can fill up that empty spot inside. In Jesus' name, amen.

THE PRAYERS FOR THE LOST

WHO'S ON YOUR LIST?

Grab an index card and write down the names of five people who don't know God. They might be family or friends. They can be young or old. They can live close by or far away. It could even be someone you've met only once or have seen only on TV. Each day, pray that they will see God at work in their lives and will decide to trust Jesus as their Savior. To help you remember to pray, put the card where you'll see it every day—like on your nightstand or tucked into your Bible. When they decide to follow Jesus, don't forget to thank God!

REMEMBER . . .

One of the best ways to love someone is to pray—and pray first—for them to know God!

WHAT DO YOU THINK?

1. How is praying for someone to know God one of the best ways to love them?

   _____

   _____

   _____

   _____

2. Look around you at school and in your community. What are people using to fill that empty spot inside? What's one way you can show them how much God loves them?

   _____

   _____

   _____

   _____

THE PRAYERS FOR THE LOST

3. Read Matthew 18:12–13 again. What do these verses tell you about God and His love for all people?

_____

_____

_____

_____

_____

_____

_____

_____

_____

_____

_____

_____

CHAPTER 11

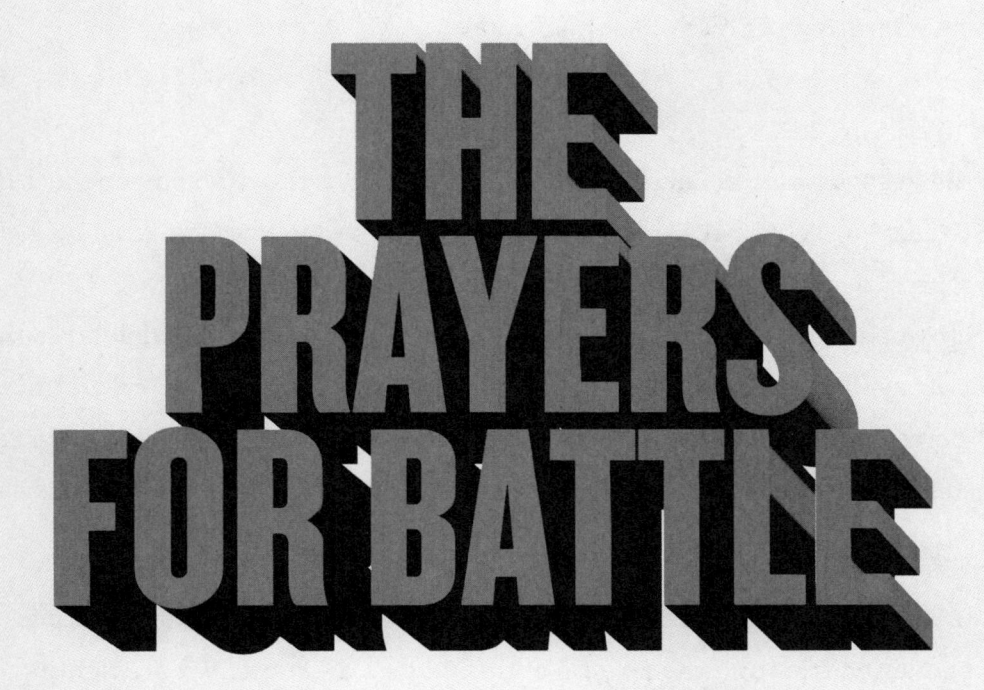

THE PRAYERS FOR BATTLE

IF YOU WANT TO MAKE SATAN WORRY, PRAY!

The Enemy doesn't like it when you partner with God and start sharing His good news and praying. Not one bit. He'll try to stop you. In fact, he'll throw everything he can at you. Little problems, big problems, busyness, a fight with a friend, sickness, and sadness—the Enemy will use it all to try to trip you up. Some days will feel like running through an obstacle course while dodging flaming arrows!

On those days (and every day!), remember that God is stronger than the devil and bigger than anything he can throw at you. God can defeat it all, and He'll give you the wisdom and strength you need to defeat it too.

Before you begin your day, pray first. Pray for yourself, and don't be shy about asking others to pray for you too. The more prayers, the better!

INVISIBLE ATTACKS

The Bible says that the Enemy is prowling around looking for someone just like us (1 Peter 5:8). Why? Because we believe in, trust, and follow God—and we try to get others to do the same. That makes us a target for his attacks.

It can be tough to spot those attacks because they're often invisible. Sounds a bit crazy, doesn't it? Well, here's something that sounds even crazier but is 100 percent true: An invisible spiritual realm is all around us. The apostle Paul called it the "heavenly realms" (Ephesians 6:12 NIV). That's where the Enemy likes to fight his battles. Check out what else Paul said:

> Our fight is not against people on earth. We are fighting against the rulers and authorities and the powers of this world's darkness. We are fighting against the spiritual powers of evil in the heavenly world. (Ephesians 6:12)

KNOW YOUR ENEMY

1. **THE DEVIL IS REAL.** He's not imaginary, but one of his greatest tricks is getting people to think that he doesn't exist.
2. **THE DEVIL WANTS TO TAKE YOU OUT.** Not out for ice cream or a burger either. He wants to take you out of the battle and away from God. He's constantly plotting and trying new ways to steal away your joy and peace and purpose. Take him seriously and fight him with your prayers.
3. **THE DEVIL IS NOT ALL-POWERFUL.** Yes, he has some power, but it's nothing compared to the power of God. The devil trembles at the name of Jesus.

It's called *spiritual warfare*. And while it might sound like something out of the movies, it's very real.

ENEMY LINES

The good news is, you're not in this fight alone. When you pray, you call upon the power of God to protect you. He will fight for you. In fact, He's already won! (The devil knows he's lost, but he just won't stop fighting.)

> **SPIRITUAL WARFARE:** the battles fought between good and evil—between God and the Enemy—in the invisible, heavenly realms

New News?

Maybe this is the first time you've heard about spiritual warfare. Maybe you're thinking, *But I'm just a kid. I'm still in school. I can't even drive yet. Do I really have to fight spiritual battles?* The answer is yes. The Enemy doesn't care about how old you are or whether or not you can drive. He's already on the attack.

Okay, that sounds a little scary. You don't have to be frightened or overly alarmed, but you must take spiritual warfare seriously. And don't worry if it's new to you. Because it's not new to God. He's the ultimate fighting expert.

Now, let's get your training started.

ARMOR FOR THE FIGHT

During His time on earth, Jesus showed us how to fight the devil: with God's Word. After Jesus was baptized, the Enemy tempted Him three times. (Read all about it in Matthew 4 and Luke 4). After each temptation Jesus repeated God's Word and used it like a sword—the sword of truth—to defend Himself. You can do the same!

GOD'S ARMOR FOR YOU

Ephesians 6:11–18 is a great checklist for making sure you're ready to defend yourself from the Enemy's attacks.[1] It's called the armor of God, and you'll want to suit up every day with each part:

- **BELT OF TRUTH:** Choose to tell the truth and believe God's truth. Remember, the devil is the "father of lies" (John 8:44).
- **BODY ARMOR OF RIGHTEOUSNESS:** This is the righteousness of Christ. His perfect holiness acts like body armor to cover and protect your heart.
- **GOOD-NEWS SHOES:** Shoes protect soldiers' feet from traps. In spiritual warfare, the good news of Jesus protects you from the Enemy's traps.

GET ARMED FOR THE FIGHT

God's Word is like a sword. You can fight off the Enemy's lies with God's true Word. But if you don't know God's Word, you can't use it in a spiritual battle.

Start arming yourself today with God's truth. Grab a journal or notebook and start collecting verses that will help you fight off the Enemy's lies and attacks. Whenever you find a new, helpful verse, write it down. Then, one at a time, start memorizing the verses so you can quickly "pull out your sword" when you need it. Here are a few to look up and get you started:

- John 16:33
- Psalm 27:1
- Romans 8:37
- Isaiah 41:10
- Isaiah 54:17

- **SHIELD OF FAITH:** The devil shoots flaming arrows of doubt, discouragement, gossip, and lies that "burn" your heart and feelings. But faith in Jesus—trusting and believing in Him—acts like a shield. Those arrows bounce right off!
- **HELMET OF SALVATION:** Knowing that Jesus loves you and has saved you is like a helmet that protects your mind and thoughts. It lets you see what is true and what is a lie of the Enemy.
- **SWORD OF THE SPIRIT:** This is God's Word. While the other armor pieces protect you, the sword of the Spirit is your weapon for attacking the Enemy.
- **PRAYER:** Take your battles to God in prayer, and trust Him to fight for you. (Spoiler alert: God always eventually wins.)

Thank You, God, for the gift of Your armor. Wrap Your truth around me like a belt. Protect my heart with Your righteousness. Help me take the good news of Jesus with me wherever I go. Shield me from the Enemy's fiery arrows. Protect my mind from attacks and fill up my thoughts with Your Word. Help me to remember that I have your armor when I need it most. I know You are bigger and stronger than anything the Enemy can throw at me. You've already defeated him. I trust You to help me defeat him too. In Jesus' name, amen.

IT'S TIME TO BE SERIOUS

When you call on the name of Jesus, you can overcome anything the devil throws at you. Not because of what you do but because the Lord will fight for you.

PRAY FIRST

These battles are serious, so pray serious prayers. Don't waste your time with wimpy prayers. Instead . . .

- **BE BOLD.** Declare that You *know* God is willing and able to fight for you and win.
- **BE SPECIFIC.** Tell God exactly what you need.
- **BE CONFIDENT.** Know that Jesus hears you and that He answers you.

DID YOU KNOW . . . ?

Logos (LO-goes) is the Greek word for *word*.[2] It's also a name for Jesus because John 1:1–4 calls Jesus "the Word" or *Logos*.

God, You promise to fight for me. I believe that You will, and I believe that You will win. You will drive the Enemy out of my home and my school. You will chase him away from my family and friends and away from me. I declare that he is not able to defeat me because You have already defeated him. You are always with me and always protecting me. One day, even the Enemy will bow before Jesus. I praise You, Lord, for giving me a place in Your kingdom. I will worship You, Lord—and only You—all the days of my life. In Jesus' name, amen.

PRAYER OF PROTECTION

When you know the Enemy is out there, it's only natural to wonder how he's going to attack. It might even worry you. That's okay. God understands those feelings. That's why He invites you to come to Him right away with any worries or

THE PRAYERS FOR BATTLE

fears. Pour out your heart to Him—everything you're thinking and feeling. Ask Him to protect you, and know that He will do it.

Remember these promises:

- "The Lord is faithful. He will give you strength and protect you from the Evil One" (2 Thessalonians 3:3).
- "He will order his angels to protect you wherever you go" (Psalm 91:11 NLT).
- "The LORD always keeps his promises" (Psalm 145:13 NLT).

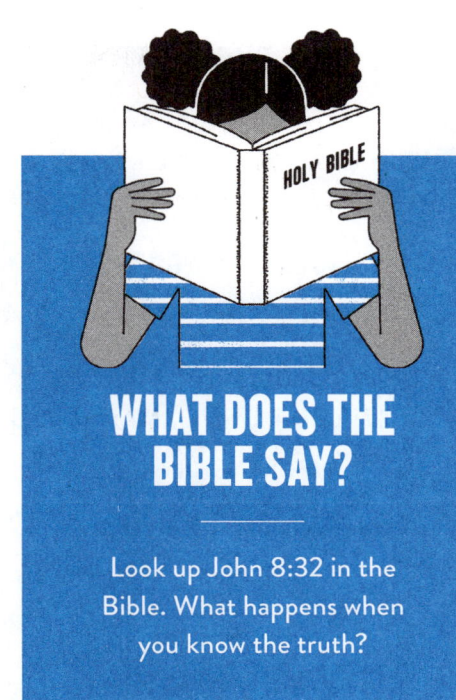

WHAT DOES THE BIBLE SAY?

Look up John 8:32 in the Bible. What happens when you know the truth?

Abba Father, thank You for how You watch over me. Please protect me and the people I love. Keep us safe as we go to school and work and everywhere else. Watch over our homes. Keep us healthy and safe. Defeat the Enemy, Lord, and every trick and trap he tries. And most of all, keep us close to You. In Jesus' name, amen.

HOW TO SPOT THE ENEMY'S LIES

The Enemy likes to sneak his lies into your thoughts. Here's how to spot them:

STEP 1: Consider what you're thinking about.

STEP 2: Compare it to what God says in His Word.

STEP 3: If it's a lie, toss it out and think about God's truth instead.

PRAY FIRST

WINNING THE FIGHT

You can be sure the Enemy has a battle plan. That means you need one too. Start with these three strategies:

1. **SUBMIT TO GOD EVERY DAY.** That means to put your trust in Him and follow Him. Even when you don't completely understand His plans. When you stick close to God, the devil can't stand it and runs away (James 4:7).
2. **DON'T LEAVE ANY DOORS OPEN IN YOUR LIFE THAT MIGHT LET THE ENEMY SNEAK INSIDE.** Huh? Think of it this way: If you left the doors of your home unlocked, a thief could walk right in and steal your stuff. Well, if you disobey God and ignore His commandments, you leave the door wide open for the devil to walk right in and steal your peace, joy, and strength to fight him. Close and lock that door by obeying God.
3. **PULL OUT YOUR SWORD OF TRUTH—GOD'S WORD—AND USE IT EVERY DAY.** Keep your sword sharp by reading it. Use it to slice through the Enemy's lies and remind yourself of the good and true things God says.

DON'T FORGET!

God's Spirit, who is in you, is greater than the devil, who is in the world.
—1 John 4:4

AN ELEPHANT AND THE DEVIL

There's a legend about a circus elephant who was tied in its pen with only a thin rope. It could have easily snapped that rope and gotten free. But it never even tried. Why?

When the elephant was young, the trainers

THE PRAYERS FOR BATTLE

used a heavy chain to keep it in its pen. It tried and tried to escape, but the elephant could never break the chain. Soon, it stopped trying. From then on, the trainers only needed a thin rope to keep the elephant in its pen because the elephant *believed* it was still bound by that unbreakable chain.

The devil wants to do the same to you. He tells you lies and pretends he has real power. He tells you that he's in control and is the boss of you. But it's all a lie. (He's a really good liar.) If you listen to him, you'll be like that elephant tied up with a tiny rope. Break out your sword of truth—God's Word—and break free of those lies.

REMEMBER . . .

No matter how you're feeling or what you're going through, the power of God is only a prayer away. He will give you the strength and power you need to defeat the Enemy's attacks and live as a follower of Christ—when you pray first!

WHAT DO YOU THINK?

1. Does the Enemy keep trying to get you to believe a certain lie? Maybe about who you are or who God is? Pull out your sword (Bible) and find a truth to defeat that lie. (Ask a grown-up for help if you need to.)

_____

_____

_____

PRAY FIRST

2. Is it hard for you to pray boldly? If you said yes, what is holding you back?

   _____

   _____

   _____

   _____

   _____

3. Psalm 145:13 says that God always keeps His promises. What does that tell you about how God will fight for you?

   _____

   _____

   _____

   _____

   _____

CHAPTER 12
THE PRAYER FOR YOU

WHEN YOU PRAY, GOD ANSWERS—SOMETIMES WITH "YES," SOMETIMES WITH "NO," AND SOMETIMES WITH "NOT YET."

DEEP IN THE DESERT

The "salt pan" in Death Valley, California, is the hottest, driest place in the entire United States. In the summer, temperatures often reach higher than 120 degrees Fahrenheit.[1] And rain? Forget about it! Death Valley only gets about two inches of rain *a year*. Nothing grows there. Not trees, not bushes, not flowers—nothing.

But about once every ten years, it does rain. Then, the next spring, something wonderful happens. Wildflowers bloom! A carpet of yellow, purple, and pink blossoms covers the valley. It's called a "super bloom."

For years these wildflower seeds lie just under the soil, waiting for enough

PRAY FIRST

water to sprout and bloom. Then, when conditions are just right, they bloom! These wildflowers are proof that life—beautiful life—can happen even in the most hopeless situations.

Especially when you pray first.

YOUR BEST LIFE

The path to your best life starts with prayer. Because your best life starts with God. Check out this prayer from the apostle Paul. It's for believers just like you:

I always remember you in my prayers and always thank God for you. . . . I pray that he will give you a spirit that will make you wise in the knowledge of God—the knowledge that he has shown you. I pray that you will have greater understanding in your heart. Then you will know the hope that God has chosen to give us. I pray that you will know that the blessings God has promised his holy people are rich and glorious. And you will know that God's power is very great for us who believe. That power is the same as the great strength God used to raise Christ from death. (Ephesians 1:15, 17–20)

Paul's prayer breaks down into four parts:
- To know God better
- To receive understanding
- To discover your purpose
- To make a difference

DON'T FORGET!

By his divine power, God has given us everything we need for living a godly life.
—2 Peter 1:3 NLT

THE PRAYER FOR YOU

It's a prayer you can pray for both yourself and others. Let's take a closer look at these four parts.

KNOW GOD

Paul asked God to give believers "a spirit that will make you wise in the knowledge of God" (Ephesians 1:17). That's a fancy way of asking God to help you know Him better.

Faith starts with knowing God. Of course, getting to know God isn't a one-and-done kind of thing. It's not like learning the multiplication tables, and then there's nothing else to know. You'll be learning things about God your whole life. Because He's infinite and all-powerful. And because . . . He's God!

This kind of knowing isn't just knowing facts *about* Him either. After all, you can know facts about the king of England but never meet him.

DID YOU KNOW . . . ?

The apostle Paul (also known as Saul) was one the greatest missionaries for God ever. But there was a time when he hated Christians so much that he went around arresting them—and worse! Then Paul saw the light. Literally! (Read about it in Acts 9.) He then went out on the road (and the ocean) to tell everyone about Jesus. He started churches, and he wrote letters to encourage and teach those churches. The book of Ephesians is one of those letters.

Instead, this kind of knowing is like knowing your best friend—what they like on their burger, what their favorite song is, what hurts their feelings, and what they dream about doing when they grow up.

Knowing God is the most important mission you'll have in your whole life. It's

HOW TO KNOW GOD

Spend time alone with Him, being still and quiet and listening, doing some of these things:

- Read His Word.
- Sing praises to Him.
- Worship Him.
- Talk to Him (that is, pray).
- Listen to Him.

The more you get to know Him, the more you'll want to know.

more important than learning about Him, serving Him, or praising Him. And it starts when you remember to pray first!

> Holy Father, I want to know You. Yes, I want to know about You, but I also want to know You and Your heart—even better than I know my parents or my best friend. Please show me something new about who You are today. In Jesus' name, amen.

GET UNDERSTANDING

Paul prayed, "I pray that you will have greater understanding in your heart. Then you will know the hope that God has chosen to give us" (v. 18). Or, to say it a little more simply: Keep "your eyes focused and clear, so that you can see exactly what it is he is calling you to do" (vv. 17–18 THE MESSAGE).

Understanding what God wants you to do is an amazing thing. It gives you a purpose for your life, helps you see how you should live, and helps you grow stronger in your faith.

THE PRAYER FOR YOU

You May Need to Clean Out Your Heart First

Before you can get that kind of understanding in your heart, though, you may need to clean out a few other things first.

You see, your heart can be like your closet. It's easy to shove stuff in there and shut the door—even stuff you know you should just throw away. You might have a grudge or two stuffed in there, along with a box full of selfishness, some old pride, and even some sins that you've been hiding and hoping no one would find.

Ask God to help you clear out all that stuff—and He absolutely will. But it's also good to have a group of friends who will help you and pray for you. Make sure these friends are trustworthy and love both you and God. They should be ready to encourage you but also not be afraid to tell you when you're wrong and need to make some changes.

When you have friends like that, you can "confess your sins to each other and pray for each other . . . so that God can heal you" (James 5:16).

Because what's better than praying first? Praying first together!

> Lord, please show me the things that I've hidden away in my heart—the things that don't belong there. Help me to clean them out. In Jesus' name, amen.

DISCOVER YOUR PURPOSE

Why are you here? Not in your room or wherever you happen to be at this moment. But why are you on earth? Why are you in this time and place and with these people instead of somewhere in South America in the 1600s?

PURPOSE: what God wants you to do for Him and His kingdom

PRAY FIRST

Sooner or later, everyone wonders what their purpose is. As a follower of God, your purpose is big—bigger than getting rich or popular or being the first to download the latest version of your favorite game.

God has a job for you to do: a purpose. And He's given you gifts and talents to help you accomplish that purpose (Romans 12:6–8). Your gifts and talents won't be quite like anyone else's. Just like your purpose will be unique to you.

Figuring out what gifts God has given you and how to use them will take a little time and a little experimenting. Start by thinking about what you enjoy, what makes you excited, and what makes you feel closer to God. Maybe you love doing one of these things:

- Helping with events and setting things up
- Working with lights or sound
- Teaching younger kids
- Singing
- Reading to the sick
- Writing stories or letters
- Drawing out Bible lessons and characters
- Volunteering at a food bank or shelter

WHAT DOES THE BIBLE SAY?

Look up 1 Peter 4:10 in the Bible. What should you use your gifts to do?

THE PRAYER FOR YOU

Don't be afraid to try out a few different ways of serving others. After all, you can't go wrong if you're serving God!

WHAT ARE YOUR GIFTS?

Figuring out the gifts God has given you can take a little time—and your gifts can change over time. But try starting here.

STEP 1: Ask God.

STEP 2: Make two lists. In one, write down the things you're good at. In the second, write down the things you enjoy doing for others or the church. Did something pop up on both lists? It could be one of your gifts.

STEP 3: Ask others what they think you're great at.

STEP 4: Explore and experiment. Try different ways of serving until you find the one that's the best fit for you.

STEP 5: Ask God. (Yep, again.)

Abba Father, show me how I can serve You today and every day. Help me see the gifts You've given me. And please give me the wisdom to know how and where to use them. In Jesus' name, amen.

MAKE A DIFFERENCE

When you start using the gifts God has given you (for His purpose for you), you will start making a difference in the world. Or at least your corner of it.

A part of your purpose is always going to be helping others know God. The Bible calls this "bearing fruit" (John 15:5 NIV), and it makes God so incredibly happy.

Something else happens when you focus on using your gifts to serve God and others—you'll be happier too. Your troubles and struggles won't seem quite so important. Some of them may even disappear completely. Instead of worry and fear, your heart will be filled with joy.

> *Abba Father, You are so good, and You are so good to me. I want to share Your goodness with others. Help me use the gifts You've given me to make a difference in the world. In Jesus' name, amen.*

REMEMBER . . .

Pray this kind of prayer for yourself, and pray it for others. It will keep you focused on God and getting closer and closer to Him. Because this isn't just a prayer that you pray or even that you pray first—it's a prayer you live!

WHAT DO YOU THINK?

1. *Your best life starts with prayer.* Do you agree? Why?

   _____
   _____
   _____

2. Why is knowing God better than just knowing about Him?

   _____
   _____
   _____

3. What do you think one of your gifts might be? How can you use it for God today?

   _____
   _____
   _____

PART 3

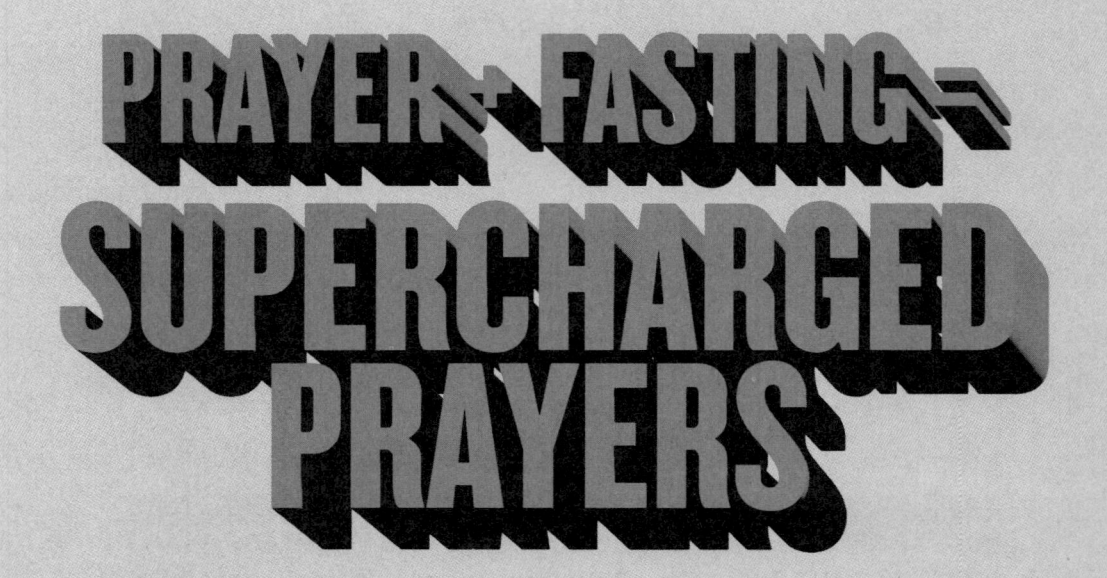

PRAYER + FASTING = SUPERCHARGED PRAYERS

WHEN YOU'RE READY TO LEVEL UP

Fasting. Maybe you've heard the word before, or maybe you haven't. Fasting has nothing to do with speed or racing. But it has everything to do with God and prayer.

Some people say fasting was just for Bible times or for monks and missionaries.

**FASTING UNPLUGS YOU FROM THE WORLD.
PRAYER PLUGS YOU BACK INTO GOD.**

They're wrong, of course. It's for anyone who wants to take their prayers to the next level.

So if you're ready to level up your prayers, let's get the facts about fasting.

CHAPTER 13

FASTING? WHAT'S THAT?

FASTING GETS RID OF THE CLUTTER AND MAKES ROOM FOR GOD.

SO, WHAT IS FASTING?

Fasting is giving something up so you can focus more on God. It's a powerful spiritual discipline—a sort of training tool to supercharge your faith. Most people think of fasting as completely giving up food—maybe for a meal, a day, or even longer.

Here's the thing, though: Right now, your body is growing so fast that it needs the fuel of nutritious foods to be healthy. That doesn't mean you can't or shouldn't fast. Because you definitely can and should. It's just going to look a little different.

You see, fasting isn't just about food. You can fast from anything that has become a go-to for comfort, entertainment, or escape. It's a way to say no to yourself and the stuff of this world so you can say yes to God more.

The Supercharge for Your Prayers

How does fasting supercharge your prayer life? By making more room for God. Imagine this:

You're studying for a huge test. In the middle of the cafeteria. Kids are yelling all around you and bumping your chair. Then someone spills their drink right next to your book. *So. Many. Distractions!* Who could focus with all that going on?

Now imagine slipping off to a corner of the library and putting on some headphones. Instead of yelling kids, you hear the sound of soothing ocean waves. No bumped chairs. No spilled drinks. So much easier to focus, right?

That's what fasting does for your relationship with God.

FASTS THAT AREN'T (REALLY) FOOD

- Junk food (like chips, sweets, or fast food)
- Sugary sodas and drinks
- Music and movies
- Video games
- Television
- Social media
- Shopping
- Texting

When You Want to Give In

When you fast, you'll be tempted at some point to grab that bag of chips (or your phone or whatever you've given up for your fast). That's when you stop and ask God to help you stay strong. (He will!) This teaches you to depend on God and trust Him to get you through.

> **SPIRITUAL DISCIPLINES:** things you do to grow closer to God, such as reading and studying the Bible, memorizing verses, giving, prayer, and fasting

Meat, Not Milk

Babies feast on milk, right? But you're not a baby. So imagine if the only food you had was milk, how hungry would you be? Starving! Your body now needs more than milk to keep growing.

The same is true for your faith. You won't grow in your faith if you just coast along on a little bit of God, reading your Bible when you have time and saying a prayer when you need a little pick-me-up. That's just "milk." It's time to get serious about your faith. It's time for a steak! "Chow down" on daily Bible reading, memorizing Bible verses, praying first, *and* fasting.

Three Parts, One You

You are made up of three parts (kind of like the God who created you). Those three parts are body, soul, and spirit. Because your body is the part you can see, it's easy for your body—your emotions and the things you crave (like ice cream)—to rule your heart and soul and choices.

Fasting takes your focus off what your body wants so you can keep your eyes on Jesus, which is the ultimate goal.

PRAY FIRST

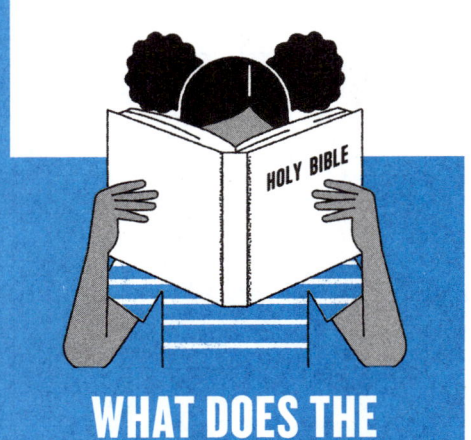

WHAT DOES THE BIBLE SAY?

Look up Matthew 6:16–18 in the Bible. What should you *not* do when you fast? What should you do instead? (Don't try to look miserable so others will notice how "holy" you are. Instead, brush your hair and wash your face so your fasting is between you and God.)

WHAT'S THAT GOAL AGAIN?

The ultimate goal of fasting (and prayer and all those other spiritual disciplines) is to sin less and to become more and more like Jesus. Will you ever be perfect like Him? No, not on earth. But with the Holy Spirit's help, you *can* be set free from wanting and choosing to sin.

Fasting makes more room for God and His Holy Spirit to work in your life. It gives you the space to make sure your heart matches up with God's. In other words, do the things you're doing and saying line up with what He wants you to do and say?

As you learn to live with less of your desires, you'll have more of God's desires in your life.

A STORY OF FAITH AND FASTING

There's a story in the Bible that shows how important fasting was to Jesus.

Jesus sent His disciples into the world to teach and heal others. And they did a lot of that. But then they met a father and his son. This son was possessed by a demon, and the disciples couldn't get rid of it. The boy's father refused to give up, though. He went straight to Jesus. Check out what Jesus said to His disciples:

"You people have no faith. Your lives are all wrong. How long must I stay

FASTING? WHAT'S THAT?

with you? How long must I continue to be patient with you? Bring the boy here." Jesus gave a strong command to the demon inside the boy. Then the demon came out, and the boy was healed. (Matthew 17:17–18)

Two Problems

Jesus' disciples couldn't get rid of that demon because they had two problems:

1. Not enough faith. ("You people have no faith.")
2. Too much world. ("Your lives are all wrong.")

The disciples' faith in God had grown weak. They weren't spending enough time with Him. (And they didn't even have the internet or crazy cat videos on YouTube to distract them!) The disciples were so busy doing things *for* God that they forgot to grow their faith *in* God. That weak faith meant they didn't have God's full power working in their lives. And without His full power, they couldn't get rid of that demon.

CHECK YOUR FAITH

How's your faith in God? It's easy to get filled up with the stuff of this world and let God get

DON'T FORGET!

Search me, God, and know my heart; test me and know my anxious thoughts. See if there is any offensive way in me, and lead me in the way everlasting.
—Psalm 139:23–24 NIV

pushed out of your life—or stuck in a corner and forgotten about until it's time for church again. So it's good to stop and check your faith every once in a while. Ask yourself these questions:

• Do you read your Bible only if you have time and after you get everything else done?

• Do you pray only when you need something?

• Are you on fire for God on Sunday mornings but fizzle out and forget Him by Monday afternoon?

DID YOU KNOW...?

What do Moses, Esther, Daniel, David, Anna, Paul, and Jesus all have in common? They all fasted! In fact, fasting is mentioned in the Bible more than seventy times!

If you answered yes to any of these questions, it's time to fix your faith!

THE FIX

Jesus gave His disciples the way to fix their broken faith and reconnect with God:

"This kind does not go out except by prayer and fasting." (Matthew 17:21 NKJV)

If you need to reconnect with God too, the answer for you is prayer and fasting.

Prayer is your direct connection to God. You don't have to check with anyone else first or get permission to talk to Him. You don't have to wait in line or make an appointment. God is always ready to listen, and talking to Him reminds you how much you need Him.

Add in fasting to supercharge your prayers and speed up that reconnection. It helps you focus *and* make more room for God. Giving up things for God isn't a punishment—it's a gift. Because getting more of God in your life is way better than any junk food, screen time, or shopping trip could ever be!

FILLING UP THAT EMPTY SPOT

In chapter 10, we talked about how there is an empty spot inside every person—including you—that only God can fill up. Sometimes people (even some who love and follow God) try to fill it with other things, though.

Fasting is a way to get rid of those other things you use to fill up that empty spot. Things like junk food, entertainment, social media, goofy videos—whatever you're counting on for comfort and pleasure to help you feel better or keep you entertained.

Fasting removes those things and makes room for more of God.

REMEMBER . . .

Fasting isn't something to ignore just because you're a kid. It's a powerful tool that will strengthen your faith, supercharge your prayers, and bring more of God, His presence, and His power into your life. So don't be slow about this . . . go fast!

> Lord, I want more of You in my life. I want to give fasting a try. Help me say no to myself and yes to You. In Jesus' name, amen.

WHAT DO YOU THINK?

1. Had you ever heard of fasting before reading this chapter? What did you think fasting was all about? What does it truly mean?

___
___
___
___
___
___
___
___
___
___

FASTING? WHAT'S THAT?

2. How could fasting help you draw closer to God?

   _____

   _____

   _____

   _____

   _____

3. What is one thing you could fast from this week—for the whole week?

   _____

   _____

   _____

   _____

   _____

CHAPTER 14

WHAT ARE FAQS ABOUT FASTING?

**FASTING ISN'T ABOUT FOOD.
IT'S ABOUT YOUR HEART.**

BUT FIRST, WHAT ARE FAQS?

FAQs are "frequently asked questions." And you've still got some questions about fasting, right? That's good! Let's find some answers.

WHY FAST?

You have plenty of right reasons to fast and one really wrong one. The Bible warns about that wrong reason in James 4:3. It's when "you want things only so that you can use them for your own pleasures." In other words, it's thinking

SOME GREAT REASONS TO FAST

- You need healing from pain.
- You need a miracle—for God to make the impossible possible.
- You need to see God working in your life.
- You need help to say no to something wrong.
- You have a God-size dream—one that only He can make happen.

only of yourself and not caring about what God wants or what might be best for others.

Make sure you're fasting for a good, pure reason, such as growing closer to God.

HOW DO YOU FOCUS ON GOD WHILE YOU FAST?

How exactly do you focus more on God? Try these tips:

- Start each day by declaring how much you need God. It can be as simple as: "Good morning, God. I need Your help today."
- Ask God to forgive you for any wrong things you've done or said. And then praise Him for forgiving you.
- Say God's name if you get distracted by the world or tempted by that thing you're fasting from. Saying His name will put your thoughts back on Him.
- Ask God to open your eyes to see Him—maybe not face-to-face, but to know that He is with you and working.
- Believe God will answer. Be specific and ask God for things only He can make happen. Then expect specific answers. Don't just hope for them. *Look* for them.

- You need the courage and the right words to talk to someone who doesn't know Jesus.
- You want God to show you what to do in a difficult situation.
- You need help figuring out what God wants you to do with your time, talents, and life.

DO YOU NEED TO CLEAR OUT THE CLUTTER?

Life can be a little bit like your school locker. It might start out neat and organized, but then it gets all cluttered. You're in a rush to meet your friends, so you just toss your books inside. Some papers fall out of your folder, but you're too busy to tuck them back in. Already you've stuffed your gym clothes, an old lunch sack, and last week's science project in there. Soon your locker is a wreck!

In the same way, selfish and sinful things can clutter up your life before you know it. Fasting is a time to clear out all the junk that doesn't draw you closer to God. The more stuff you clear out, the more room you'll make in your life for the goodness of God.

ARE THERE DIFFERENT KINDS OF FASTS?

Yes! There are basically four different kinds of fasts, so talk to God and pick the one that's right for you. *But*—and this is so incredibly important!—don't try any fast involving food until you talk to your parents and maybe even a doctor.

No-Food Fast

This kind of fast might be the one you think of first. It's a *complete fast* from all solid food. If you have to chew it, you don't get to have it. You can only have liquids, like water or sometimes juice.

WHAT DOES THE BIBLE SAY?

Look up Matthew 4:1–5 in the Bible. When did the devil come to tempt Jesus?

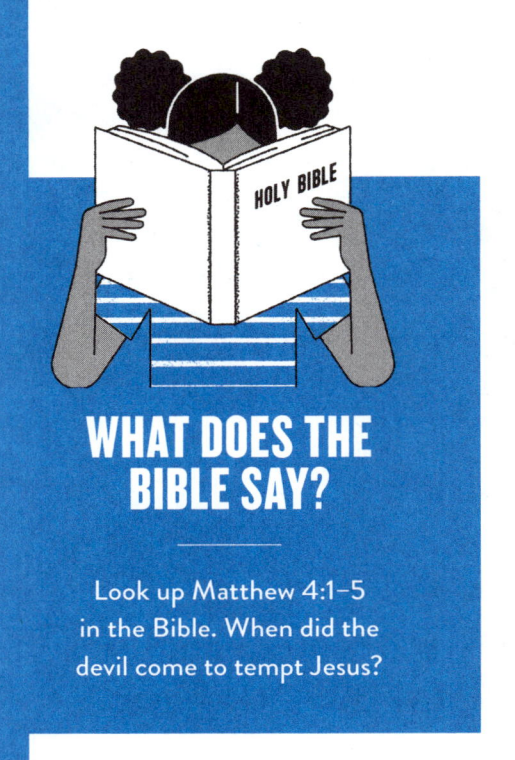

The complete fast isn't for everyone, especially if they have health struggles. And it's not for you—at least not yet. Your body is still growing and needs the fuel of nutritious, solid food. (But keep it in mind for when you're all grown up.)

For-a-Time Fast

A *partial fast* is when people fast for a certain time. Perhaps they fast all day and then only eat one meal in the evening. They then use breakfast and lunchtimes for prayer and Bible reading instead of eating. (*Again, because you're still growing, this one isn't a good idea for you.*)

A partial fast can also be from things that aren't food. Maybe you give up watching TV unless it's with your family, or maybe you give up video games except for one day a week. Then, all the time you spend watching TV or playing video games can be used for prayer or reading your Bible.

This-Not-That Fast

The next kind of fast is a *selective fast*, which means you fast only from certain foods. Sometimes it's called the Daniel Fast because that's what Daniel and his friends did when they were taken as captives to Babylon (Daniel 1:8–16). Maybe you give up sugary foods, chips, sodas, or your favorite snack.

Like the partial fast, you can do this with items other than food. For example, give up screens and spend the time reading instead.

WHAT ARE FAQS ABOUT FASTING?

Soul Fast

Instead of fasting from food, a *soul fast* means giving up comfort, pleasure, or entertainment. Perhaps you give up social media, movies, television, video games, or even all screen time. Or perhaps you give up shopping or a hobby. The goal is to step away from something you usually do and step toward God by using that time for prayer and Bible reading. Remember, fasting is about your heart, not your stomach.

> **HOLY:** to be set aside by God for His purposes and plans[1]

WHAT SHOULD YOU EXPECT WHEN YOU FAST?

No matter what kind of fast you choose to do, expect results.

- **EXPECT TO BE HEALED.** It might be healing for your body, or it might be healing for a broken heart, broken relationship, or something that's just not quite right in your life. Just remember, sometimes God will take away the pain, and sometimes God will help you see the pain as a way to grow closer to Him.
- **EXPECT TO MEET GOD'S HOLINESS AND RIGHTEOUSNESS.** When you seek God, He will come to meet you.
- **EXPECT GOD TO SET YOU BACK ON THE RIGHT TRACK.** If you've been struggling with gossip, neglecting God, making lousy choices, or having trouble being a good friend, God will guide you back to where you need to be.
- **EXPECT GOD'S HELP.** Sure, God asks you to do some tough stuff—like forgive and love your

> **HOLINESS:** the awesome wonder, power, and perfection of God

enemies. And His plans for you aren't always easy. But God is eager to help when you ask.

EXPECT TO BE SURPRISED. God isn't boring. He is creative and has unlimited power. Expect to be filled with His Spirit and for His answers to come in wonderful, surprising ways.

YOU'RE READY TO FINISH YOUR FAST. NOW WHAT?

First, don't finish a fast too fast.

Fasting changes both your body and your spirit, so be careful when it's time to end—or *break*—your fast.

For example, if you've fasted from sweets, now isn't the time to scarf down an entire king-size candy bar. Start slow with just a bite or two. Or, if you've fasted from screens, it's probably not a good idea to binge-watch an entire series. In other words, just take it slow.

Next, don't let your guard down. At the end of a fast, you may feel like you're on top of the world and untouchable—that practically dares the devil to *try* to touch you. Just because your fast is ending, don't stop praying for protection.

DID YOU KNOW...?

The word *breakfast* comes from the 1400s Middle English word *brekfast* or *breken fast*.[2] It means to break one's fast. What fast? The one from last night's dinner until this morning's *break*fast.

WHAT ARE FAQS ABOUT FASTING?

You don't want to lose that closeness to God you've gained. Give it a chance to soak all the way through your life.

WATCH WHAT YOU WATCH

For the next week, watch what you watch. In other words, grab a notebook and jot down how much time you spend on screens—whether it's a phone, tablet, computer, or television.

At the end of the week, add it all up. Does the number surprise you? What would happen if you spent just half of that time with God instead?

Father God, when I seek You, You promise that I will find You. Thank You for that! Please guide me as I seek You, and don't let the Enemy distract me or pull me away. In Jesus' name, amen.

WHAT DO YOU THINK?

1. Think about your life right now. What's one reason you should fast? If you're not sure, ask God to show you.

   _____

   _____

   _____

   _____

   _____

   _____

   _____

   _____

WHAT ARE FAQS ABOUT FASTING?

2. How could a soul fast help you focus on God? What would you fast from?

_____

_____

_____

_____

_____

_____

3. Why is it important to break your fast slowly?

_____

_____

_____

_____

_____

CHAPTER 15

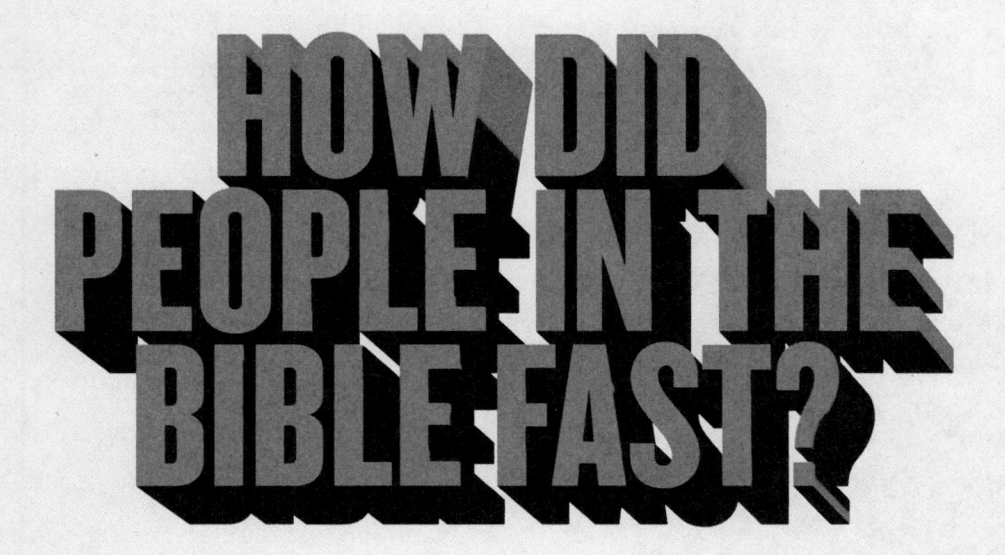

HOW DID PEOPLE IN THE BIBLE FAST?

FASTING MAKES YOUR FAITH STRONGER.

WHEN YOU FAST . . .

You might not hear as much about fasting today, but in Bible times, it was a pretty common part of their prayers and worship. In fact, when Jesus talked about fasting, He said, "*When* you fast," not *if* you fast (Matthew 6:16 NIV).

Fasting pops up many times in the Bible, but there are roughly nine different reasons people fasted and why you might want to fast too. Let's take a look at each one.

PRAY FIRST

#1: WHEN YOU'RE ABOUT TO DO SOMETHING FOR GOD

After His baptism but *before* starting His public ministry, Jesus fasted for forty days and nights in the wilderness (Matthew 4:1–17; Mark 1:12–13; Luke 4:1–14). At the end of those forty days, the Enemy decided to attack. He wanted to stop Jesus' ministry before it got started.

The devil failed, of course. But here's what you need to know: When you're about to do something for God, expect the Enemy to attack. If you're about to invite a friend to church, be on the lookout for a fear of rejection. Or if you're about to volunteer to help with VBS, don't be surprised if the Enemy whispers, *You're just a kid. You can't do that.*

Don't be afraid of the Enemy's attacks, but be ready for them. Prepare yourself with prayer and fasting to remind you to count on God because He's in control, and He'll take care of you.

#2: WHEN YOU NEED TO MAKE A DECISION

If you need to make a big decision and aren't sure what to do—or even if you think you *do* know what to do—it's always a good idea to pray first. When you add fasting to your prayers, it helps you hear God's voice more clearly. That's what the apostles Paul and Barnabas did when they chose new church leaders (Acts 14:23).

DON'T FORGET!

So our hope is in the Lord. He is our help, our shield to protect us. We rejoice in him. We trust his holy name.
—Psalm 33:20–21

Think of it this way: Have you ever been listening to a radio station—the old-fashioned kind, not the streaming kind—and suddenly, there was more static than music? The problem is that you got too far from the radio tower and the source of the music. That's similar to what happens with God. If you get too far away from Him, it's hard to hear His voice over all the other noise in your life. Fasting draws you closer to God and clears away the static.

#3: WHEN YOU NEED GOD'S PROTECTION

When the Israelites were finally set free from their captivity in Babylon, they had to travel over nine hundred miles to get back home. That's like traveling from Florida to Washington, DC!

Nine hundred miles with no cars, no planes, no hotels, and no restaurants along the way. Just lots and lots of people walking. Through strange lands. With enemies all around. So the people fasted and prayed to God for protection while they traveled (Ezra 8:21).

Whether you're going on a big trip or facing something that's a little (or a lot) scary, add fasting to your prayers for God to keep you safe.

#4: WHEN BIG EMOTIONS HIT

When David heard about King Saul's death and his friend Jonathan's death, he was heartbroken. He wept and prayed and fasted—even though their deaths meant he would now be king (2 Samuel 1:12).

When the big emotions of life hit—like sadness or anger or sorrow—turn to God and ask Him to comfort you and give you His peace. Fasting supercharges the connection between you and God so you can receive even more of His comfort and peace.

> **REPENT:** to turn away from sin and turn back to God[1]

#5: WHEN YOU'VE MESSED UP

In the book of Jonah, you'll find a great example of the I-messed-up-big-time kind of fasting. You see, the people of Nineveh were doing just about every kind of wicked thing they could think of. So God sent Jonah to warn them: Change your ways, or else. That's when the people of Nineveh realized they had messed up big time! Everyone, from the king to the poorest peasant, fasted and prayed. God saw that they were sorry and had repented. He decided not to destroy them. *Whew!*

If you've messed up (or want help to avoid messing up), pray and fast. It lets God know you're serious about wanting to be forgiven and close to Him again.

#6: WHEN YOU NEED A WIN

One time the Israelites fought one of their own tribes: the tribe of Benjamin. It seemed impossible for either side to win. The Israelites needed this battle to

WHAT FASTING DOES AND DOESN'T DO

Fasting is a super powerful tool, but here are some things fasting isn't and doesn't do:

- Fasting doesn't mean God owes you an answer.
- It doesn't mean you're right. It's possible to fast and disobey God at the same time—the Israelites did that all throughout the Old Testament!
- Fasting isn't about what *you're* giving up; it's about *who* you're inviting into your life.

end quickly before more of God's people were killed. So they fasted and prayed—and God ended the battle the very next day (Judges 20:26–36).

When it seems impossible to win, when you don't see any way out, when the enemy you're facing is big and scary—that's when you need God's help to win. That's also when you need to pray—and then supercharge your prayers by fasting.

#7: WHEN YOU WANT TO WORSHIP GOD

Anna was eighty-four years old. She "never left the Temple but stayed there day and

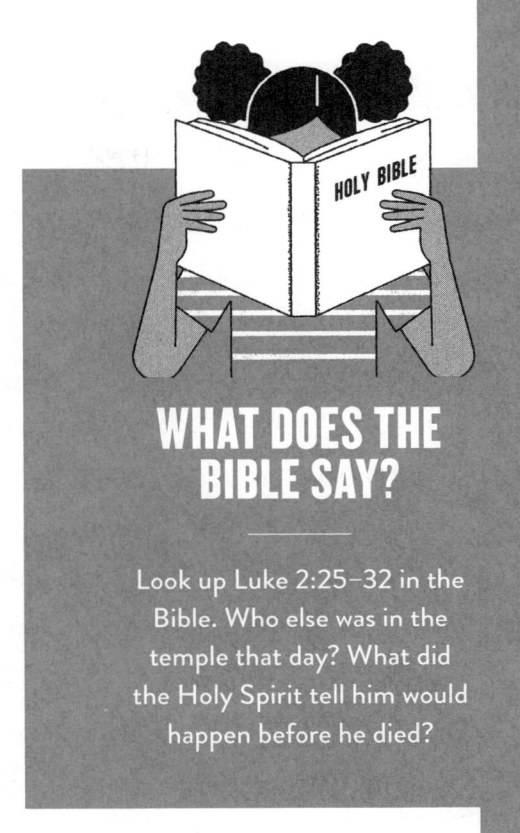

WHAT DOES THE BIBLE SAY?

Look up Luke 2:25–32 in the Bible. Who else was in the temple that day? What did the Holy Spirit tell him would happen before he died?

But here is what fasting does:

- Fasting unplugs you from this crazy, busy world that steals your time, energy, and attention.
- Fasting pulls you closer to God.
- Fasting helps you listen to God's Holy Spirit as He shows you things you need to work on and ask forgiveness for.
- Fasting helps you understand and soak up more of God's Word.
- Fasting lets you fall even more in love with God as you see who He is and all He does for you.
- Fasting makes your faith bolder so you can't wait to tell others how much Jesus loves them.

night, worshiping God with fasting and prayer" (Luke 2:37 NLT). When she saw Mary and Joseph bring baby Jesus to the temple, she knew all her prayers for a Savior to rescue the people had been answered. And she had even more reasons to worship and praise God.

God is the only One worthy of your worship. Worship Him with words and songs. Worship Him with your prayers. And show Him that He has first place in your life by worshiping Him with a fast.

#8: WHEN YOU'RE DESPERATE AND ONLY GOD CAN HELP

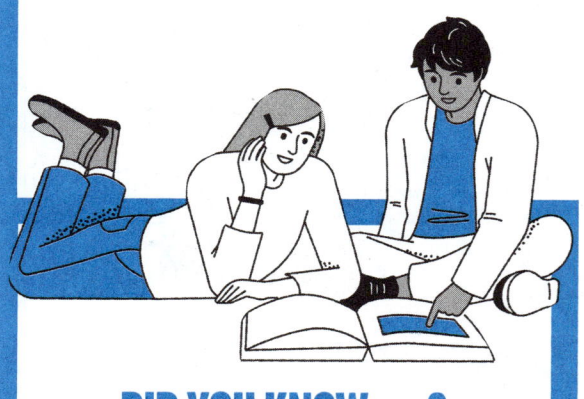

When the Israelites were exiled to Babylon, the king chose a young Hebrew woman named Esther to be his queen. One day, Queen Esther learned about a plan to kill all the Jews. She needed to talk to the king. But if she went to see him without an invitation, Esther could be killed.

Esther prayed and fasted, and she asked all the Jews to pray and fast with her for three days. Then Esther went to see the king, and God made a way for His people to be saved (Esther 2–7).

Desperate times like Esther's call for desperate measures—and fasting may be the best desperate measure

DID YOU KNOW...?

Anna was a prophetess. She had been married for only seven years when she became a widow. She then lived in the temple and devoted her life to serving God. Because Anna was so close to God, she immediately recognized the baby Jesus as the Savior.

of all. As you know by now, prayer should be the very first thing you do when trouble comes. But there might be times when you want to do more. That's when fasting can help you focus on your prayers to God and listen for His answers.

ALL TOGETHER NOW

Want to get others to pray and fast with you like Esther did? Now, that's supercharging your prayers to the max! Give it a try.

STEP 1: Gather a group of your friends or family—or both—and choose a time when you will all pray and fast together.

STEP 2: Decide what you will pray for. Perhaps you want to pray for someone who doesn't know Jesus, someone who needs healing, or a specific need. Or maybe it's just to tell God how awesome and amazing He is!

STEP 3: Decide what you will give up for your fast. You can all give up the same thing. Or each person can fast from something different.

STEP 4: Decide how long you will fast.

STEP 5: Check in on one another and encourage one another during the fast.

STEP 6: When it's over, get together and talk about how you and the things you were praying for have changed.

STEP 7: Praise God!

#9: WHEN YOU'RE FIGHTING A SPIRITUAL BATTLE

Right after Paul talked about the armor of God (see chapter 11), he said: "Pray in the Spirit at all times. Pray with *all kinds of prayers*, and ask for everything you need. To do this you must always be ready. Never give up. *Always pray for all God's people*" (Ephesians 6:18, emphasis added).

Did you notice that? Paul said, "all kinds of prayers." *Fasting* is a kind of prayer—and when you add it to your prayers, it calls even more of God's power into your life. You can ask God to cover you *and* those around you in spiritual armor against the Enemy's attacks and lies.

All nine of these reasons for fasting have one thing in common: counting on God!

REMEMBER . . .

There's nothing magical about fasting. When you fast, the Holy Spirit uses your fasting to strengthen your faith and make you more like Jesus. Fasting simply clears away everything else so you can focus on God and your relationship with Him.

> Abba Father, no matter what I'm facing—whether I need protection or guidance when making a decision or help handling a big emotion—remind me to turn to You. Teach me to add fasting to my prayers so I can have even more of You and Your power in my life. In Jesus' name, amen.

WHAT DO YOU THINK?

1. Which of these nine reasons for fasting fits your life right now? How might a fast help you?

   _____

   _____

   _____

   _____

   _____

2. Look back at the section called "When You Need to Make a Decision." What sorts of "static" creep into your life?

   _____

   _____

   _____

   _____

   _____

PRAY FIRST

3. What could you fast from that would clear away some of that static—at least for a little while? Write out a plan for how and when you would do that fast. Jot down notes about what your prayers should be.

_____

_____

_____

_____

_____

_____

_____

_____

_____

_____

CHAPTER 16

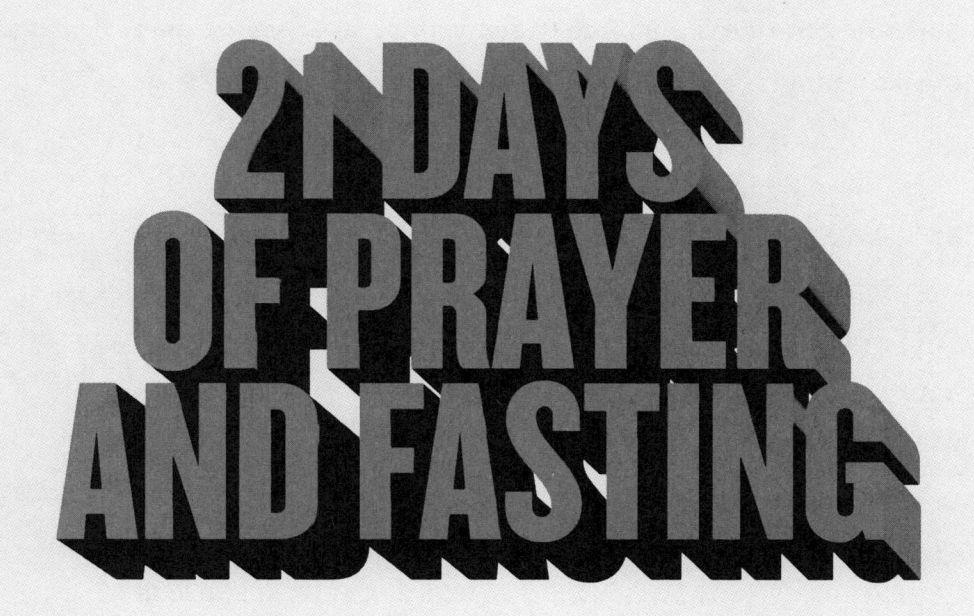

21 DAYS OF PRAYER AND FASTING

WHEN YOU NEED HELP, TALK TO GOD. HE'S NEVER TOO BUSY FOR YOU.

RIGHT FROM THE START

A great way to start off your year (or school year or anytime you want to get closer to God) is with a twenty-one-day fast. Why twenty-one days? Because that's how long Daniel fasted in the Old Testament (Daniel 10:3). If it's good enough for Daniel, it's good enough for us, right?

EVERYDAY PRAYERS

Twenty-one days can be a *loooong* time. What will you pray about for all those days? Here are some ideas. Feel free to add your own! These things are great to include in your prayers every single day.

1. **BE HUMBLE:** God, forgive me for my sins.
2. **SEEK GOD:** Lord, I want You to be first in my life at home, at school, with my friends, and everywhere I go.
3. **PRAY THAT GOD'S KINGDOM WILL COME:** Father God, please use me to shine Your love into the world.
4. **ASK TO HEAR FROM HEAVEN:** God, I pray that You'll work in my life, my school and church, my home and community, and in this country. Work in such ways that the whole world will know You are Lord!
5. **BELIEVE GOD WILL ANSWER YOUR PRAYERS FOR YOUR SPECIFIC NEEDS:** God, I feel ____, and I worry that ____. I think I need ____. But You know what is best and always do what is best. I will trust You to take care of me.
6. **PRAY FOR OTHERS:** Lord, please open the heart and eyes of ____. Help them to know You too.

21-DAY PRAYER JOURNAL

Journal the twenty-one days of prayer, making a list of the things you pray for each day. At the end of the twenty-one days, go back and reread your prayers. Make a note of any answers you've already seen—or how your prayers changed.

21 DAYS OF PRAYER AND FASTING

You can do these twenty-one days alone, of course, but it's even more wonderful and powerful when you pray through them with others. It will not only draw you all closer to God, but it will also draw you closer to each other.

Week 1: All About Jesus

SUNDAY: THE LORD'S DAY

Go to church, rest, and think about the gift of Jesus.

> Remember to keep the Sabbath as a holy day (Exodus 20:8).

What does rest for your body look like for you?

_____

_____

_____

_____

_____

Lord, thank You for encouraging me to rest. Today I ask You to help my body rest.

_____

_____

_____

_____

_____

PRAY FIRST

MONDAY: COUNT ON JESUS

Look for all the ways Jesus is already working in your life.

> "You will not succeed by your own strength or by your own power. The power will come from my Spirit," says the Lord of heaven's armies (Zechariah 4:6).

What do you see Jesus doing in your life? How is He changing your heart and your actions?

_____
_____
_____
_____

Jesus, thank You for never leaving me to figure things out on my own. Help me to . . .

_____
_____
_____
_____

TUESDAY: GIVE YOUR LIFE TO GOD

Give control of every part of your life to God. Follow His plan for your life and obey Him so you can be closer to Him and more like Jesus.

> "I want your will to be done, not mine" (Matthew 26:39 NLT).

What is one thing you can do or say today to be more like Jesus?

_____
_____
_____

God, please help me to be a little more like Jesus every day.

_____
_____
_____

WEDNESDAY: WORSHIP THE LORD

Worship the Lord for who He is, and praise Him for all He's done for you.

> I will praise the Lord at all times. His praise is always on my lips (Psalm 34:1).

Think of all Jesus has done for you. What stands out to you most?

_____
_____
_____

Jesus, Your love for me is amazing. I especially love the way You . . .

_____
_____
_____

THURSDAY: CONFESS YOUR SINS

Tell God about all the wrong things you've done and the mistakes you've made—and then believe He has forgiven you through Jesus.

> God, you will not reject a heart that is broken and sorry for its sin (Psalm 51:17).

God's love for you is so huge that He sent Jesus to make a way for you to be forgiven for your sins. How does that make you feel about choosing to do what's right?

_____

_____

_____

_____

> God, please show me the sins that are in my life. Please forgive me for . . .

_____

_____

_____

_____

FRIDAY: LISTEN TO THE GOOD SHEPHERD

Be still with your Good Shepherd. Listen for His voice.

> He brings all of his sheep out. Then he goes ahead of them and leads them. They follow him because they know his voice (John 10:4).

What does a shepherd do for his sheep? What does Jesus, the Good Shepherd, do for you?

_____
_____
_____
_____

Lord Jesus, You are the Good Shepherd. I'm so grateful for the way You . . .

_____
_____
_____
_____

SATURDAY: TELL HIM ALL YOUR TROUBLES

Talk to the Lord about everything that is troubling you, and trust Him to take care of you.

> Depend on the Lord. Trust him, and he will take care of you (Psalm 37:5).

Did you know that you can tell Jesus anything? What is something you'd like to tell Him today?

_____
_____
_____
_____

PRAY FIRST

Lord Jesus, thank You for always listening to me. Today I want to share . . .

_____
_____
_____
_____

Week 2: God's Work in You

SUNDAY: THE LORD'S DAY

Go to church, rest, and think about all the good things God does for you.

Remember to keep the Sabbath as a holy day (Exodus 20:8).

What does rest for your mind look like for you?

_____
_____
_____
_____

Lord, thank You for encouraging me to rest. Today help my mind rest by . . .

_____
_____
_____
_____

MONDAY: FREEDOM

Thank God for the freedom from sin and worry that Jesus gives you.

> We have freedom now because Christ made us free. So stand strong (Galatians 5:1).

How does knowing that God is always with you help you not to worry?

_____
_____
_____
_____
_____

God, I'm so grateful that You are always with me. I know You will . . .

_____
_____
_____
_____
_____

TUESDAY: YOUR RELATIONSHIPS

Pray for the important people in your life, such as family and friends.

> First, I tell you to pray for all people. Ask God for the things people need, and be thankful to him (1 Timothy 2:1).

PRAY FIRST

Who are the people in your life who need your prayers?

_____

_____

_____

_____

God, I know that You love my family and friends even more than I do. Please be with . . .

_____

_____

_____

_____

WEDNESDAY: GROWING IN FAITH

Ask God to help your faith grow stronger and bolder.

> Lord, we are your servants. Help us to speak your word without fear (Acts 4:29).

Are you ever afraid to talk to others about God? What makes you afraid?

_____

_____

_____

_____

Lord, I don't want to be afraid to tell others about how awesome You are. Help me to be bold by . . .

_____
_____
_____

THURSDAY: YOUR CALLING

God has given you a mission—a job to do for Him and His kingdom. Thank Him for that mission and for the gifts He's given you to do it.

> God chose you to tell about the wonderful things he has done. He called you out of darkness into his wonderful light (1 Peter 2:9).

God wants you to work with Him to tell others about Jesus. What does "work with Him" mean to you? What is one way you can do that today?

_____
_____
_____

God, thank You for the way You made me and for giving me all my gifts, talents, and skills. Please show me . . .

_____
_____
_____
_____

FRIDAY: HEALING

Praise God for all the ways He's healed you in the past. Ask Him to touch and heal any broken or hurting places in your life now.

> Christ carried our sins in his body on the cross. He did this so that we would stop living for sin and start living for what is right. And we are healed because of his wounds (1 Peter 2:24).

What is causing you pain in your life right now? Or in the lives of those you love?

_____
_____
_____
_____

God, You are the perfect Healer. I lift up this pain to You and pray that . . .

_____
_____
_____
_____

SATURDAY: YOUR BLESSINGS

Thank God for all the blessings and good things He's poured into your life.

> I said to the Lord, "You are my Lord. Every good thing I have comes from you" (Psalm 16:2).

Every good thing comes from God, but those good things aren't just "stuff" you can see. What other good things does God give you?

_____
_____
_____

God, I can't even count all the good things You've given me. But today I'm especially thankful for . . .

_____
_____
_____

Week 3: God's Work in Others

SUNDAY: THE LORD'S DAY

Go to church, rest, and think about how God wants all people to love and follow Him.

Remember to keep the Sabbath as a holy day (Exodus 20:8).

What does rest for your heart and emotions look like for you? Why do you need to be rested to help others?

_____
_____
_____

PRAY FIRST

Lord, thank You for encouraging me to rest. Today I ask You to help my heart and emotions rest by . . .

_____
_____
_____

MONDAY: LEADERS

Pray for leaders, such as your parents, school leaders, church leaders, and government leaders.

> You should pray for kings and for all who have authority. Pray for the leaders so that we can have quiet and peaceful lives—lives full of worship and respect for God (1 Timothy 2:2).

Who are the leaders in your community and world? Who can you pray for today?

_____
_____
_____
_____

Father God, I pray for those who are leaders. Please help them to love You and . . .

_____
_____
_____
_____

TUESDAY: MISSIONARIES AND MINISTERS

Pray for all those serving as missionaries and ministers—those here at home and those far away.

> "The Holy Spirit will come to you. Then you will receive power. You will be my witnesses—in Jerusalem, in all of Judea, in Samaria, and in every part of the world" (Acts 1:8).

Who are the ministers in your church? Are there missionaries? What is one way you can help them?

_____
_____
_____
_____

Lord, be with those who tell others about You. Help them . . .

_____
_____
_____
_____

WEDNESDAY: YOUR CHURCH

Ask God to bless your church, its leaders, your pastor, and all the members.

> And you are helping us by praying for us (2 Corinthians 1:11 NLT).

PRAY FIRST

Think of all the different people who work at your church. How do they help you draw closer to God?

_____
_____
_____
_____

God, please guide our church leaders. Fill them with Your words and . . .

_____
_____
_____
_____

THURSDAY: GROWN-UPS

Pray for all the grown-ups in your life, especially those closest to you.

> First, I tell you to pray for all people. Ask God for the things people need, and be thankful to him (1 Timothy 2:1).

Who are the grown-ups in your life? Who helps you? Who teaches you about Jesus? Who needs your prayers?

_____
_____
_____
_____

Father God, thank You for the people You've put in my life to help me. Please teach me to . . .

_____

_____

_____

FRIDAY: THE LOST

Pray for those who don't know Jesus as their Lord and Savior. Ask God to open their hearts to Him.

> The Lord is not slow in doing what he promised—the way some people understand slowness. But God is being patient with you. He does not want anyone to be lost. He wants everyone to change his heart and life (2 Peter 3:9).

Who is someone in your life who doesn't follow Jesus? How can you talk to them about Jesus? How can you show them you love Jesus—without saying a word about Him?

_____

_____

_____

God, teach me what to say and do so I can tell others about You. I especially want to . . .

_____

_____

_____

SATURDAY: THE VICTORY

Thank God for all the wonderful and incredible things He has shown you over the last twenty-one days.

> But we thank God! He gives us the victory through our Lord Jesus Christ (1 Corinthians 15:57).

God is always working in your life—loving you, protecting you, teaching you, and listening to you. How do you feel about that?

_____
_____
_____
_____

God, You are just so amazing! I've learned so much about being Your child these last few days. Thank You for . . .

_____
_____
_____
_____

REMEMBER . . .

As you pray through these twenty-one days, don't be surprised when the experience of talking with God gets just a little bit more wonderful every day. It will be a spiritual adventure!

To pray for yourself and others: "May the Lord bless you and keep you. May the Lord show you his kindness. May he have mercy on you. May the Lord watch over you and give you peace" (Numbers 6:24–26).

WHAT DO YOU THINK?

1. What did you choose to fast from for these twenty-one days? How did you do it? Would you do it the same way next time, or would you do something different?

   _____

   _____

   _____

   _____

2. Was fasting easier or harder than you thought it would be? Did your feelings about the fast change as the days went by?

   _____

   _____

   _____

3. How did fasting affect your prayers? How did it affect your relationship with God?

_____

_____

_____

_____

_____

_____

4. If a friend wanted to do a twenty-one-day fast, what advice would you give them?

_____

_____

_____

_____

_____

_____

CHAPTER 17

DO YOU HAVE YOUR SHIELD?

I WILL SAY TO THE LORD, "YOU ARE MY PLACE OF SAFETY AND PROTECTION. YOU ARE MY GOD, AND I TRUST YOU."
—PSALM 91:2

GOD'S SHIELD

Many places in the Bible talk about God being a shield around His people, like this verse from Psalm 3: "Lord, you are my shield. You are my wonderful God who gives me courage" (v. 3).

How do you get God's shield to cover your life? Just ask! (How easy and awesome is that?)

PRAYER SHIELD: when others lift you up to God and cover you with their prayers like a shield

You're Gonna Want More Shields

But when you face the Enemy—and let's face it, we all do—you will want as many shields as possible to cover you, right? You will want prayer shields.

What's a *prayer shield*? It's when other people pray for you. Their prayers cover you like a whole bunch of shields. And your prayers cover them like a shield too. Because just like fasting can supercharge your prayers, gathering with others to pray multiplies the power of your prayers and unleashes God's Spirit to work in mighty ways.

BUILD YOUR OWN PRAYER SHIELD

STEP 1: Invite other people to pray for you and with you. These people are called *prayer warriors*.

STEP 2: Decide when to meet to share praises and prayer requests, such as before school, at lunch, after dinner, on Saturdays, or after church. (If you can't meet in person, no problem! Put technology to work for God, and set up a group text or ask your parents to help set up a virtual meeting.)

STEP 3: Pray.

STEP 4: Keep on praying!

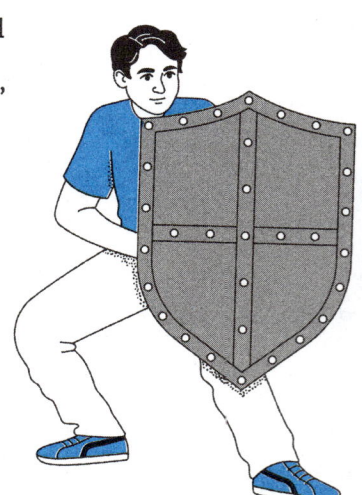

PRAYER WARRIORS' BATTLE PLAN

Okay, you've invited a group of people to pray for you and with you. You've decided on a time to meet. Now, what do you do when you meet? Here are some ideas:

- Pray first! Ask God to guide your meeting.
- Offer up some praise. Listen or sing along to some worship songs.
- Read a short devotion to focus your thoughts.
- Share any answered prayers and praises.
- Share prayer requests.
- Commit to praying for each other every day.
- Pray again and ask God to shield you all until you meet again.

REMEMBER . . .

Now is the time to put all you've learned about prayer and fasting into

DID YOU KNOW . . . ?

When Nehemiah and the Israelites returned to Jerusalem after being captive in Babylon, their city was in ruins. The walls that kept Jerusalem safe from its enemies had huge holes in them. Some parts had been completely knocked down. Since the Israelites were surrounded by enemies, they needed to rebuild those walls fast!

Those enemies planned to attack *before* the Israelites could get the walls back up. So Nehemiah and the Israelites fought them together *with their prayers*! Half the people worked on the wall, while the other half stood guard. And they *all* put their "minds on the Master" (Nehemiah 4:14 THE MESSAGE). That wall was rebuilt in only fifty-two days (Nehemiah 6:15–16)!

PRAY FIRST

practice. No worries, though. You've got this . . . or rather, God's got this, and He's got you.

Just don't forget to . . .

- Pray without stopping.
- Pray with other people.
- And always pray first!

> Abba, Father God, thank You for the gift of prayer. I'm so grateful that I don't have to worry about messing it up and getting everything just right. I can just talk to You, and I can even ask You to help me listen for Your answers. Thank You for loving me so much. In Jesus' name, amen.

WHAT DO YOU THINK?

1. How would joining with other prayer warriors help your prayer life be stronger?

   _____

   _____

   _____

   _____

2. Think back over all that you've learned about prayer. What were you surprised to learn?

_____

_____

_____

_____

_____

_____

3. What has made the most difference in your relationship with God?

_____

_____

_____

_____

_____

_____

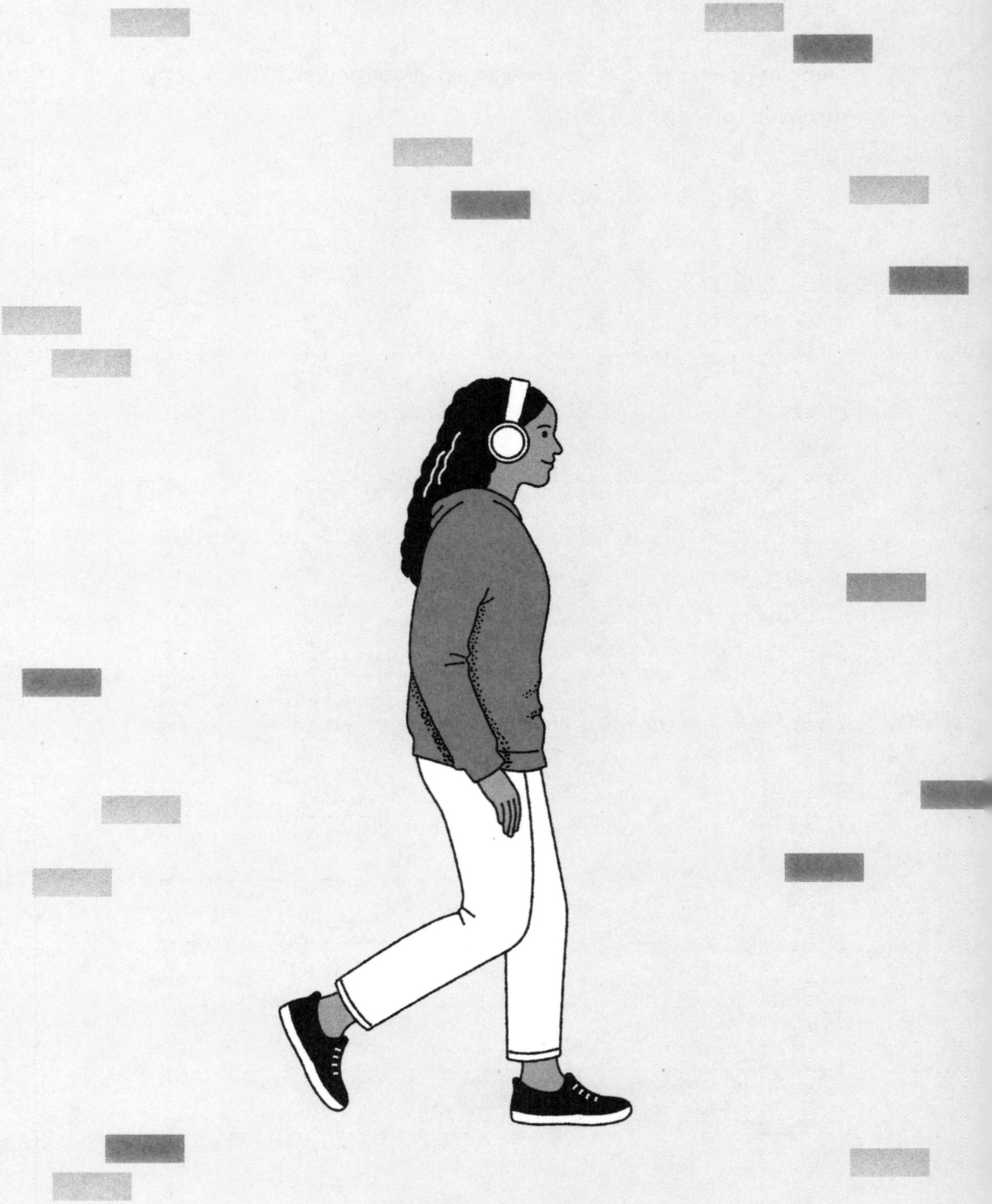

ACKNOWLEDGMENTS

To all my friends who offered support, encouragement, and assistance on this project, I am more grateful than you'll ever know. I'm especially indebted to:

My wife, Tammy: You have been so loving and supportive in everything I have ever done. You are a gift from God, and I will love you always.

My assistant, Katy Smith: I simply couldn't do what I do without your help. Thank you for your hard work and devotion. You are such a blessing to me.

My writing partner, Dudley Delffs: Thank you for being a part of my life and ministry.

My agent, Matt Yates: Thank you for the encouragement, insight, and wisdom you provided throughout this entire process. I'm so grateful for your friendship and support.

The team at Thomas Nelson: Your partnership continues to bless me. I'm especially grateful for my editor, Bri Gallagher.

My writer, Tama Fortner, and illustrator, Geraldine Sy: It was a joy to work with you.

Kellen Coldiron and Beth Cunningham: Thank you for your invaluable contributions and for making me better.

My Savior and Lord, Jesus my King: It is a privilege to be on Your team. Thank You for choosing me.

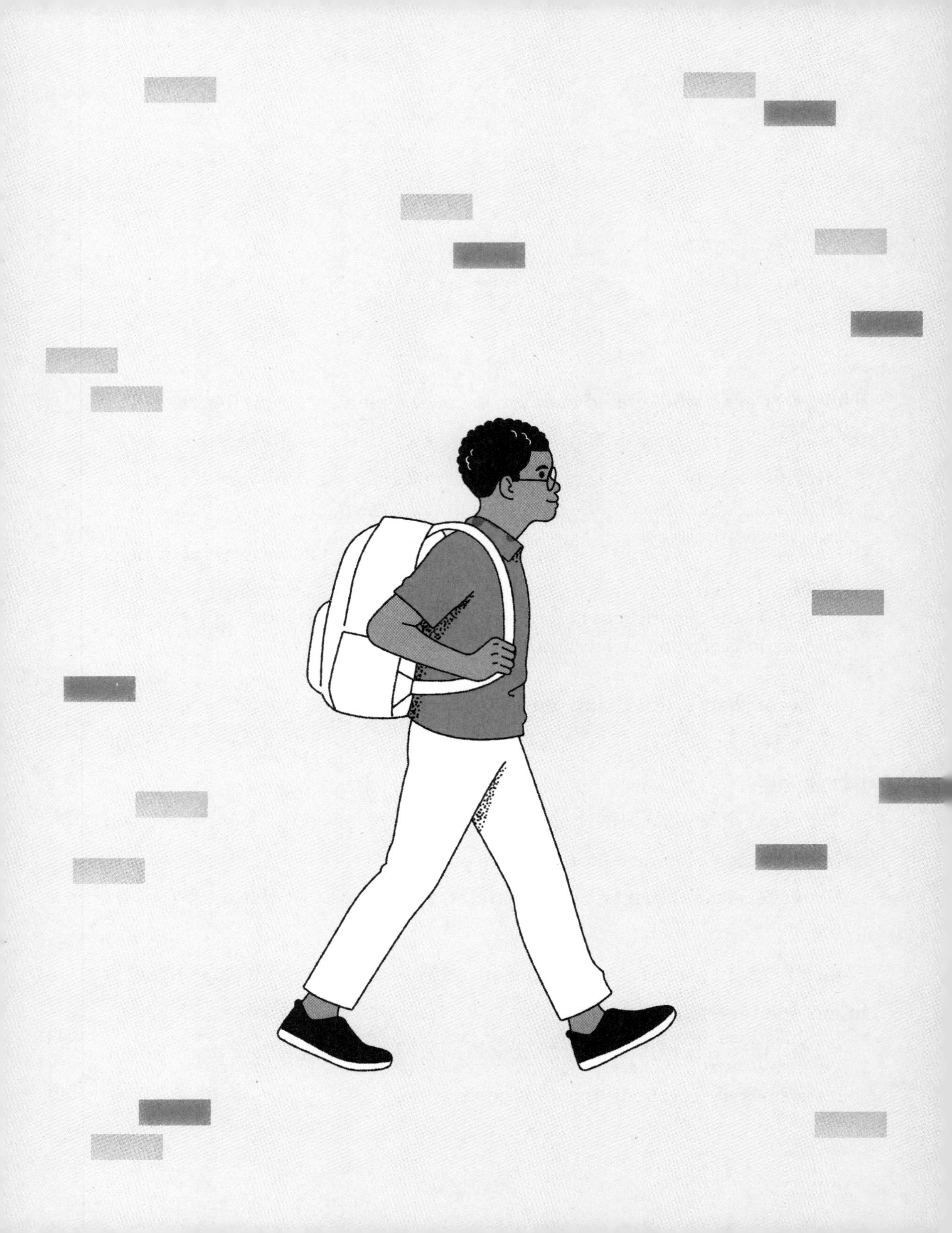

NOTES

CHAPTER 4: THE HOW OF PRAYER
1. Bible Tools, "energeo," accessed December 27, 2024, https://www.bibletools.org/index.cfm/fuseaction/Lexicon.show/ID/G1754/energeo.htm.

CHAPTER 5: THE WHO OF PRAYER
1. Bible Tools, "parakletos," accessed December 27, 2024, https://www.bibletools.org/index.cfm/fuseaction/Lexicon.show/ID/G3875/parakletos.htm.

CHAPTER 7: THE PRAYER OF MOSES
1. "What Was the Significance of the Bronze Laver?" Got Questions, https://www.gotquestions.org/bronze-laver.html.

CHAPTER 8: THE PRAYER OF JABEZ
1. Keshia Sophia Roelofs, "564 Biblical Baby Names & Meanings," Peanut, January 4, 2024, https://www.peanut-app.io/blog/biblical-baby-names.
2. Blue Letter Bible, "barak," accessed December 27, 2024, https://www.blueletterbible.org/lexicon/h1288/kjv/wlc/0-1/.

CHAPTER 9: THE PRAYER OF THE SHEEP
1. "What Is Righteousness?" Got Questions, https://www.gotquestions.org/righteousness.html.

CHAPTER 10: THE PRAYERS FOR THE LOST
1. "What Does It Mean That Believers Are to Be Salt and Light (Matthew 5:13–16)?" Got Questions, https://www.gotquestions.org/salt-and-light.html.
2. *Merriam-Webster Dictionary*, "wisdom," accessed December 27, 2024, https://www.merriam-webster.com/dictionary/wisdom.

NOTES

CHAPTER 11: THE PRAYERS FOR BATTLE
1. "What Is the Full Armor of God?" Got Questions, https://www.gotquestions.org/full-armor-of-God.html.
2. "What Is the Logos?" Got Questions, https://www.gotquestions.org/what-is-the-Logos.html.

CHAPTER 12: THE PRAYER FOR YOU
1. "Death Valley: Weather," National Park Service, updated May 2024, https://www.nps.gov/deva/planyourvisit/weather.htm.

CHAPTER 14: WHAT ARE FAQS ABOUT FASTING?
1. "What Does the Bible Say About Holiness?" Got Questions, https://www.gotquestions.org/holiness-Bible.html.
2. *Merriam-Webster Dictionary*, "breakfast," accessed December 27, 2024, https://www.merriam-webster.com/dictionary/breakfast.

CHAPTER 15: HOW DID PEOPLE IN THE BIBLE FAST?
1. "What Does It Mean That God Repented?" Got Questions, https://www.gotquestions.org/God-repented.html.

PRAYER NOTES

PRAYER NOTES

PRAYER NOTES

PRAYER NOTES